I0009914

AI-900 Exam
Preparation
Guide

Dedication

This book is dedicated to all the aspiring AI professionals, IT specialists, data scientists, and students who are embarking on their exciting journey into the world of artificial
intelligence. Your curiosity, dedication, and passion for learning inspire us. This guide is crafted to equip you with the knowledge and skills necessary to not only pass the Microsoft AI-900 exam but also to confidently navigate the ever-evolving landscape of AI and its applications within the Azure ecosystem. We celebrate your ambition and commitment to growth in this rapidly expanding field. We hope this book serves as a valuable tool in your journey, providing a solid foundation upon which you can build a successful and impactful career in AI. May this

work
empower you to leverage the
transformative potential of AI to solve
complex problems and shape a better
future. We commend your dedication
to continuous learning and
professional development; embrace
the challenges and
celebrate the successes along the way.
Your pursuit of
knowledge is a testament to your
commitment to excellence and your
potential to make significant
contributions to the AI community.
Remember, the journey of learning is
a
marathon, not a sprint, and we are
here to support you every step of the
way. Good luck!

Preface

The field of artificial intelligence is rapidly transforming industries and reshaping our world. Microsoft, a leader in the AI space, offers the AI-900 certification exam, which serves as a gateway to understanding the fundamental concepts and applications of AI within the Microsoft Azure cloud platform. This book is your comprehensive companion on this journey. We understand that preparing for the AI-900 exam can be daunting, given the breadth and depth of topics covered. That's why we've designed this guide to be both thorough and accessible. We've combined detailed explanations of core AI principles with practical, real-world examples to make learning engaging and effective. We've structured the book in a way that is easy to follow, with clear

headings, subheadings, summaries, and numerous
checkpoints to reinforce learning and maintain your
engagement. We've also included practice questions and quizzes throughout to help you assess your understanding and prepare effectively for the exam. Beyond the exam itself, we aim to provide you with a solid foundation in AI,
empowering you to apply your knowledge to real-world problems. This book is designed to support various learning styles and technical backgrounds. Whether you're an aspiring AI professional, an experienced IT professional, a data scientist, or a student, this comprehensive guide will help you acquire the knowledge and skills you need to
succeed. So, embark on this learning journey with
confidence and let this book be your trusted guide to
navigating the exciting world of AI with Microsoft Azure.

Introduction

Welcome to the world of artificial intelligence! This book serves as your guide to mastering the fundamentals of AI and preparing for the Microsoft AI-900 certification exam. The AI-900 exam is a valuable credential that demonstrates your understanding of core AI concepts and Microsoft Azure's powerful AI services. This book is designed to be a comprehensive resource, covering all the exam objectives in a clear, concise, and engaging manner. We'll delve into the essential building blocks of AI, including different types of AI, machine learning algorithms, computer vision, natural language processing (NLP), and conversational AI. A significant focus will be on responsible AI principles—a crucial aspect of ethical AI development and deployment.

We'll explore Microsoft's guidelines for responsible AI, examining fairness, reliability, privacy, inclusiveness,

transparency, and accountability. We'll also guide you

through Azure's powerful ecosystem of AI tools, including no-code/low-code solutions like Azure Machine Learning Studio and AutoML. You'll learn how to utilize Azure's services for computer vision, NLP, and conversational AI, with practical examples to make the learning process more engaging. Throughout the book, we'll emphasize the "why"behind the concepts, explaining not just what an algorithm does, but also how it works and why it's important. Real-world examples, diagrams, and summaries will help you grasp complex ideas.

We strongly encourage you to utilize Azure's free tier to gain hands-on experience with the

services described in this book. This will significantly

enhance your understanding and solidify your learning. This book isn't just about passing an exam—it's about building a solid foundation in AI that will serve you well in your career. Let's begin this exciting journey together!

Understanding the AI Exam and its Objectives

The Microsoft AI-900 exam, officially titled "Microsoft Azure AI Fundamentals," serves as a crucial stepping stone for anyone aspiring to work with artificial intelligence (AI) within the Microsoft Azure ecosystem. This exam isn't designed to test your coding proficiency; instead, it assesses your understanding of core AI concepts and how these concepts are implemented within Azure's suite of services. Passing the AI-900 demonstrates a foundational knowledge essential for various roles, from data scientists and AI engineers to IT professionals looking to integrate AI solutions into their workflows.

The exam itself is a multiple-choice test, typically administered online through a Pearson VUE testing center or a proctored online environment. The duration is approximately 90 minutes, allowing ample time to thoroughly consider each question. The questions are designed to be scenario-based, requiring you not only to recall definitions but also to apply your understanding to practical situations. This focus on application is critical, as it reflects the real-world challenges faced when working with AI. Expect questions to cover a wide range of topics, from the fundamental differences between supervised and unsupervised learning to the practical application of specific Azure AI services.

The structure of the AI-900 exam is carefully crafted to assess a comprehensive understanding across several key domains. These domains include:

Core AI Concepts:
This section lays the groundwork, covering fundamental AI definitions, the distinctions

between various AI types (narrow, general, super), and the core tenets of machine learning, deep learning, and their subtypes (supervised, unsupervised, reinforcement learning).
Understanding the strengths and weaknesses of each approach is critical. You will be tested on your ability to differentiate between these and apply the appropriate technique given a scenario.

Machine Learning Algorithms:
A grasp of essential machine learning algorithms is fundamental. The exam will assess your knowledge of regression (predicting continuous values), classification (categorizing data), and clustering (grouping similar data points) algorithms. Understanding their underlying principles and when to apply each is key.

Computer Vision:
This section delves into the world of computer vision, which empowers computers to "see" and interpret images. The exam will test your knowledge of image classification, object detection, and image segmentation. Familiarity with Azure's Computer Vision service, Face API, and Form Recognizer will be particularly important.

Natural Language Processing (NLP):
NLP focuses on enabling computers to understand and process human language. You'll need to understand concepts like sentiment analysis, text classification, named entity recognition, and language translation. Knowledge of Azure's offerings in this area—Text Analytics, Language Understanding (LUIS), Speech service, and Translator—is vital.

Conversational AI:
This section explores the creation of chatbots and virtual assistants. The exam covers the principles of conversational AI

design and the utilization of Azure's Bot Service and Bot Framework Composer.

Azure AI Services:
A significant portion of the AI-900 focuses on understanding and applying various Azure AI services. This requires familiarity with their functionalities, use cases, and how they integrate with each other.

Responsible AI:
A growing emphasis is placed on the ethical considerations surrounding AI. The exam will test your awareness of responsible AI principles, including fairness, reliability, privacy, inclusiveness, transparency, and accountability. You will be expected to understand how to mitigate bias and ensure ethical implementation.

Creating a structured study plan is crucial for success.
Consider your learning style and time constraints when designing your approach. Allocate sufficient time for each domain, focusing on areas where you feel less confident.

Begin with the foundational concepts (core AI, machine learning algorithms) before moving to the more specialized areas (computer vision, NLP, conversational AI). Use a combination of learning resources, including the official Microsoft Learn platform, online courses (Coursera, edX), and this book.

The Microsoft Learn platform provides official training materials directly from Microsoft. These modules are carefully aligned with the exam objectives and often include interactive exercises and quizzes to reinforce learning. These resources are free and easily accessible, making them an invaluable part of your study plan. Supplementing this with other reputable online courses can broaden your understanding and provide diverse perspectives on the material. Many courses offer hands-on labs and projects to solidify your grasp of the concepts.

Remember that consistent effort is key. Don't cram the night before the exam; instead, dedicate time each day or week to review the material. Use practice questions throughout your study plan to identify areas needing more attention. Many online resources offer AI-900 practice exams, providing valuable feedback and highlighting any weaknesses in your knowledge. These practice exams simulate the real exam environment, allowing you to familiarize yourself with the question format and pacing. Consider joining online study groups or forums to connect with other individuals preparing for the exam. Collaborating and discussing challenging concepts can be highly beneficial.

Beyond the technical knowledge, a successful exam strategy also involves effective time management during the test.
Familiarize yourself with the exam interface and practice navigating between questions efficiently. Read each question carefully, paying close attention to the details and what is

being asked. If you encounter a difficult question, don't spend excessive time on it. Mark it for review and move on to other questions. Once you've completed the rest, revisit any marked questions with the remaining time.

Finally, remember that the AI-900 is a stepping stone. Passing this exam signifies a foundational understanding, opening doors to more specialized learning and career opportunities within the exciting and rapidly evolving field of artificial intelligence. While mastering the technical details is important, also remember the importance of continuous learning. The field of AI is constantly evolving, with new techniques, algorithms, and services emerging regularly. Embrace the ongoing learning process and you'll ensure long-term success in this dynamic domain. The journey of mastering AI is a marathon, not a sprint. By following a well-structured plan, utilizing available resources, and maintaining consistent effort, you can

confidently approach the AI-900
exam and achieve your professional
goals. Remember to leverage
Azure's free tier

to practice hands-on with the services. This provides invaluable real-world experience that complements your theoretical understanding. The hands-on experience allows you to solidify your knowledge by applying what you have learned in a practical setting. The familiarity you gain through this practice will prove incredibly beneficial when you encounter similar scenarios in the exam.

A Foundation in Artificial Intelligence

Understanding the foundational concepts of Artificial Intelligence (AI) is paramount to success in the AI-900 exam and, more broadly, in navigating the world of AI. This section delves into the core definitions and distinctions that form the bedrock of AI, setting the stage for understanding more complex topics later in the book. Let's begin by defining AI itself. At its simplest, AI refers to the simulation of human intelligence processes by machines, especially computer systems. These processes include learning (acquiring information and rules for using the information), reasoning (using rules to reach approximate or definite conclusions), and self-correction. This broad definition encompasses a vast array of technologies and applications.

However, the term "AI" is often used interchangeably with several related concepts, sometimes causing confusion. It's crucial to understand the subtle yet significant differences between artificial intelligence, machine learning, and deep learning. While deep learning is a subset of machine learning, and machine learning is a subset of AI, understanding their distinct characteristics is vital.

Artificial Intelligence (AI) is the overarching concept – the ambition to create machines capable of performing tasks that typically require human intelligence. This encompasses a wide spectrum of approaches, including rule-based systems, expert systems, and the more advanced techniques of machine learning and deep learning. Consider a simple spam filter: This could be a rule-based AI system, identifying spam based on pre-defined criteria like the presence of specific keywords or sender addresses. This is a basic form of AI, operating on pre-programmed rules rather than learning from data.

Machine learning (ML), on the other hand, represents a significant advancement. Instead of relying on explicit programming, ML algorithms learn from data. They identify patterns, make predictions, and improve their performance over time without being explicitly programmed for each specific scenario. Imagine an email spam filter that learns to identify spam by analyzing vast amounts of labeled data (emails marked as spam or not spam). The algorithm identifies patterns in the data, such as the frequency of certain words or phrases, and uses these patterns to classify new emails. This is a much more sophisticated approach than a simple rule-based system, adapting and improving its accuracy as it processes more data.

Deep learning (DL), a subset of machine learning, utilizes artificial neural networks with multiple layers (hence "deep") to analyze data. These networks are inspired by the structure and function of the human brain, allowing them to learn complex patterns and representations from large datasets. For example, a deep learning model could be used to identify objects in images with remarkable accuracy, far surpassing the capabilities of traditional machine learning techniques.

This is because deep learning models can learn highly complex features from raw data, without the need for manual feature engineering. Consider image recognition in self-driving cars. A deep learning model can analyze images from cameras to identify pedestrians, traffic lights, and other vehicles, allowing the car to navigate safely. The complexity of the task requires the ability to learn intricate features from raw pixel data, a task that is ideally suited to deep learning.

Beyond these core definitions, it's important to differentiate between various

types

of AI based on their capabilities:

Narrow or Weak AI, General or
Strong AI, and Super AI.
Understanding these distinctions is
key to grasping the current state
and future potential of the field.

Narrow or Weak AI refers to AI
systems designed and
trained for a specific task. These
systems excel at their
designated task, but lack the ability to
generalize to other tasks. The
examples we've discussed so far –
spam filters, image recognition
systems – are all examples of narrow
AI. They are highly specialized and
effective within their limited domain,
but cannot perform tasks outside that
domain. They lack the broader
understanding and adaptability of
human intelligence.

General or Strong AI, on the other
hand, represents a
hypothetical AI with human-level
cognitive abilities. Such an AI would

possess the ability to learn, understand, and apply knowledge across a wide range of tasks, much like a human. This type of AI remains largely theoretical. While significant progress has been made in narrow AI, creating a truly general AI presents formidable challenges, requiring breakthroughs in areas such as common sense reasoning, natural language understanding, and problem-solving in complex, unpredictable environments.

Super AI is a further hypothetical concept referring to an AI system that surpasses human intelligence in all aspects. This level of AI is purely speculative, and its potential implications are a subject of ongoing debate. While some experts believe the development of super AI is inevitable, others express concerns about its potential risks, emphasizing the need for careful consideration of ethical and safety implications.

Understanding the distinctions between these types of AI is crucial, not only for the AI-900 exam but also for

responsible innovation in the field. The capabilities of current AI systems are still limited, predominantly residing within the realm of narrow AI. However, ongoing research and development are constantly pushing the boundaries, gradually expanding the capabilities of AI systems. This continuous advancement brings forth both immense opportunities and significant ethical considerations that require careful attention and responsible development practices. The ethical implications of AI, a topic we will explore in more detail later, become increasingly significant as AI systems become more powerful and capable.

The implications of AI, across all its forms, are far-reaching and transformative. From automating mundane tasks to powering groundbreaking scientific discoveries,

AI is
rapidly reshaping our world. Consider
the impact of AI in healthcare, where
AI algorithms can analyze medical
images to detect diseases earlier and
more accurately than human doctors.
In finance, AI-powered systems
manage risk, detect fraud, and
personalize financial advice. In
transportation, self-driving cars
promise to revolutionize how we
travel, improving safety and
efficiency. The possibilities seem
limitless.

However, the widespread adoption of
AI also brings about significant
challenges. The potential for bias in
AI
algorithms, the impact of AI on
employment, and the ethical
considerations surrounding
autonomous weapons systems are just
a few of the critical issues that require
careful
consideration and proactive solutions.
This necessitates a responsible
approach to AI development and
deployment, prioritizing ethical
principles and societal well-being.

To successfully navigate the complexities of AI, a solid foundation in its core concepts is essential. The distinctions between AI, machine learning, and deep learning, along with the categorization of AI into narrow, general, and super AI, provide a crucial framework for understanding the current landscape and future trajectory of this transformative technology. The AI-900 exam emphasizes this foundational knowledge, making it a crucial stepping stone for anyone seeking a career in this dynamic and rapidly evolving field. Remember that continuous learning is key in this field; new techniques and applications emerge constantly, requiring a commitment to ongoing professional development. This book will provide you with the knowledge necessary to pass the AI-900, but your learning journey should not end there.

Supervised Unsupervised and Reinforcement Learning

Building upon our foundational understanding of AI, we now delve into the heart of machine learning— the engine driving many AI applications. Machine learning algorithms are categorized broadly into three types: supervised, unsupervised, and reinforcement learning. Each type addresses different problems and uses distinct approaches to learning from data. Understanding these distinctions is critical for the AI-900 exam and for practical application in various fields.

Supervised learning is the most prevalent type of machine learning, characterized by its reliance on labeled datasets. Think of it as learning with a teacher. The "teacher" provides the algorithm with input data alongside its corresponding output, effectively guiding the learning process. The algorithm learns to map inputs to outputs by identifying patterns and relationships within the labeled data. Once trained, the algorithm can then predict outputs for new, unseen inputs.

A simple analogy is learning to identify different types of fruit. A supervised learning algorithm would be given images of apples, bananas, and oranges, each labeled with its respective name. The algorithm analyzes the visual features of each fruit (color, shape, size) and learns to associate these features with the correct label. After training, it can then correctly classify a new image of a fruit it hasn't seen before.

Common supervised learning algorithms include linear regression, logistic regression, support vector machines (SVMs),

and decision trees. Linear
regression is used for

predicting continuous values, like house prices based on size and location. Logistic regression, on the other hand, predicts categorical values, such as whether a customer will click on an advertisement (yes/no). SVMs excel at classification tasks by finding the optimal hyperplane that separates different classes of data. Decision trees create a tree-like model to classify or predict outcomes based on a series of decisions.

The success of supervised learning hinges on the quality and quantity of the labeled data. Insufficient or biased data can lead to inaccurate predictions. Consider a spam detection system trained on a dataset that predominantly contains spam emails from a specific region. This system might incorrectly flag legitimate emails from that region as spam due to the biased training data. Therefore, data cleansing, preprocessing, and careful selection of training data are crucial steps in building effective supervised learning models.

In the business world, supervised learning finds widespread application. Fraud detection systems use supervised learning to identify fraudulent transactions based on historical data of legitimate and fraudulent activities. Customer churn prediction models use supervised learning to predict which customers are likely to cancel their subscriptions, allowing businesses to proactively engage these at-risk customers. Medical diagnosis systems use supervised learning to identify diseases based on patient symptoms and medical history. These examples highlight the versatility and impact of supervised learning in various domains. The AI-900 exam will cover several specific applications and algorithms, reinforcing the practical importance of this learning method.

Unsupervised learning, in contrast to supervised learning, works with unlabeled data. There is no "teacher" providing explicit guidance; instead, the algorithm aims to discover inherent structures and patterns within the data itself. This is analogous to exploring a new city without a map—you observe your surroundings, identify landmarks, and gradually build a mental map of the city.

Clustering is a prominent technique within unsupervised learning, aiming to group similar data points together. For instance, customer segmentation uses clustering to group customers based on their purchasing behavior, demographics, or other characteristics. Businesses can then tailor their marketing strategies to specific customer segments, leading to improved efficiency and customer satisfaction. K-means clustering is a popular algorithm for this purpose, aiming to partition the data into k clusters, where each data point belongs to the cluster with the nearest mean.

Another important aspect of unsupervised learning is dimensionality reduction. High-dimensional data, containing many features, can be challenging to analyze and visualize. Dimensionality reduction techniques, such as Principal Component Analysis (PCA), aim to reduce the number of features while preserving important information. This simplifies the data, improving the efficiency and interpretability of subsequent analysis.

Anomaly detection is another crucial application of unsupervised learning, focusing on identifying outliers or unusual data points. Credit card fraud detection, for example, uses anomaly detection to identify transactions that deviate significantly from a customer's typical spending patterns. Network intrusion detection systems similarly utilize unsupervised learning to identify malicious activities in network traffic.

Unsupervised learning, while lacking the explicit guidance of labeled data, plays a critical role in exploratory data analysis, uncovering hidden patterns and insights that might otherwise be overlooked. It empowers businesses to understand their data more comprehensively and make data-driven decisions. Understanding the core techniques and applications of unsupervised learning, including clustering and dimensionality reduction, is essential for the AI-900 exam.

Reinforcement learning differs significantly from supervised and unsupervised learning. It focuses on training agents to make decisions in an environment to maximize cumulative rewards. Imagine teaching a robot to navigate a maze. The robot (agent) explores the maze, receiving rewards for reaching checkpoints and penalties for hitting walls.

Through trial and error, the robot learns the optimal path to maximize its rewards.

Reinforcement learning algorithms learn through interaction with the environment, receiving feedback in the form of rewards or penalties. The core components are the agent (the learner and decision-maker), the environment (the world the agent interacts with), and a reward function (defining the desirability of different states and actions). The agent learns a policy, which maps states to actions, by iteratively exploring the environment and maximizing its cumulative reward.

Common reinforcement learning algorithms include Q-learning and Deep Q-Networks (DQNs). Q-learning uses a Q-table to store the expected cumulative reward for each state-action pair. DQNs extend Q-learning by using deep neural networks to approximate the Q-function, allowing them to handle complex environments with high-dimensional state spaces.

Reinforcement learning has gained significant traction in recent years, finding applications in robotics, game playing, and resource management. Self-driving cars, for example, use reinforcement learning to learn optimal driving strategies in complex traffic situations. Recommendation systems use reinforcement learning to personalize recommendations based on user interactions.

The key distinction between reinforcement learning and other machine learning paradigms lies in the interactive nature of the learning process. The agent actively explores the environment, learns from its experiences, and adapts its behavior over time. This iterative process allows the agent to develop sophisticated strategies for achieving its goals.

Understanding the basic principles and applications of

reinforcement learning is essential for a comprehensive grasp of the AI landscape, particularly relevant to the AI-900 exam.

In summary, supervised, unsupervised, and reinforcement learning represent distinct approaches to machine learning, each with its unique strengths and applications. Supervised learning uses labeled data to predict outcomes, unsupervised learning discovers patterns in unlabeled data, and reinforcement learning learns through interaction with an environment. Understanding these distinctions, along with their practical applications, is crucial for success in the AI-900 exam and for navigating the complex world of AI. The practical examples provided throughout this section, emphasizing real-world business scenarios, aim to solidify your understanding and build a robust foundation for further exploration. Remember to explore Azure's free tier to gain hands-on experience with these different learning paradigms, further enriching your learning journey.

Essential Machine Learning Algorithms

Building upon our understanding of the three primary
machine learning paradigms –
supervised, unsupervised, and
reinforcement learning – we now
explore some essential algorithms that
power these approaches. These
algorithms form the core of many AI
applications and are frequently tested
in the AI-900 exam. It's vital to grasp
not just
what these algorithms do, but also
why
they are chosen for
specific tasks and their underlying
limitations. Let's begin with
supervised learning algorithms.

Supervised learning, as we've
discussed, relies on labeled datasets.
This means each data point is tagged

with the correct answer, allowing the algorithm to learn the mapping between inputs and outputs. This learning process creates a model that can predict the output for new, unseen inputs.

Two crucial categories within supervised learning are regression and classification.

Regression Algorithms:
Regression algorithms predict a continuous output variable. Think of predicting house prices based on features like size, location, and age. The output—the price—is a continuous value, not a categorical label.

Linear Regression:
This is arguably the simplest regression algorithm. It models the relationship between the input variables and the output variable as a linear equation.

Imagine plotting data points on a graph; linear regression finds the best-fitting straight line through these points. This line represents the predicted relationship. While simple,

linear regression provides a baseline and forms the
foundation for understanding more complex regression techniques. For instance, predicting the sales of a product

based on advertising spend can be effectively modeled using linear regression, assuming a linear relationship between the two. However, its simplicity means it struggles with non-linear relationships.

Polynomial Regression:
Extending linear regression, polynomial regression models the relationship using a polynomial equation. This allows it to capture more complex, non-linear patterns in the data. Imagine a curve instead of a straight line. Polynomial regression can fit this curve, enabling it to model relationships where a linear approach would fail. For example, predicting crop yields based on fertilizer application might exhibit a non-linear relationship: initially, yields increase with fertilizer, but after a certain point, increasing fertilizer can lead to

diminishing returns or even harm to the crop.

Support Vector Regression (SVR):
SVR aims to find the best-fitting hyperplane that maximizes the margin between the data points and the hyperplane. Unlike linear regression which minimizes the sum of squared errors, SVR focuses on maximizing the margin, making it robust to outliers.
Consider predicting stock prices. Stock prices often exhibit volatility and outliers. SVR's robustness to outliers makes it a suitable choice in this scenario.

Decision Tree Regression:
This algorithm builds a tree-like model where each node represents a decision based on an input variable, and each leaf node represents a predicted output value. It partitions the data into regions, each with a predicted output. Predicting customer churn based on
various factors like usage patterns, customer service
interactions, and demographics is a

good application for decision tree regression. The tree visually shows which factors are most important in driving churn.

Random Forest Regression:
An ensemble method, it combines multiple decision trees to improve prediction accuracy and robustness. Each tree is trained on a random subset of the data, and the final prediction is an average of the predictions from all trees. The randomness reduces overfitting and improves generalization, making it a powerful tool for various prediction tasks. For example, predicting customer lifetime value could benefit significantly from the robustness and accuracy offered by random forest regression.

Classification Algorithms:
Classification algorithms predict a categorical output variable. This means the output is one of several predefined categories. For example, classifying emails as spam or not spam.

Logistic Regression:
Despite its name, logistic regression is a classification algorithm. It models the probability of an instance belonging to a particular category. It's often used for binary classification (two categories) but can be extended to handle multiple categories. Predicting whether a customer will click on an advertisement, based on their demographics and browsing history, is a typical application.

Support Vector Machines (SVM):
SVMs aim to find the optimal hyperplane that separates different categories of data. They are particularly effective when dealing with high-dimensional data and non-linear relationships. Identifying fraudulent transactions based on various financial parameters is an ideal use case where SVM's ability to handle complex relationships shines.

Decision Tree Classification:
Similar to decision tree regression, but the leaf nodes represent categories instead of continuous

values. Classifying images of
handwritten digits

(0-9) is a common application where the clear decision boundaries help this algorithm perform well.

Naive Bayes:
This algorithm is based on Bayes' theorem and assumes that features are independent of each other. While this assumption is often unrealistic, it's surprisingly effective in many situations. Spam filtering is a classic example where Naive Bayes excels.

K-Nearest Neighbors (KNN):
This algorithm classifies a data point based on the majority class among its k-nearest neighbors in the feature space. It's a simple and intuitive algorithm, but it can be computationally expensive for large datasets. Recommending products to customers based on their purchase history, where similarity between customers can be measured using KNN, is a practical example.

Random Forest Classification:
Similar to random forest regression, but used for classification tasks. This ensemble method combines multiple decision trees to improve accuracy and robustness, handling complex relationships effectively. Image recognition, where many features need to be analyzed to correctly classify images, is a suitable application.

Unsupervised Learning Algorithms:
Unsupervised learning algorithms deal with unlabeled data, meaning there are no pre-defined categories or outputs. The goal is to discover patterns, structures, or relationships within the data. Clustering is a primary type of unsupervised learning.

K-Means Clustering:
This algorithm partitions the data into k clusters, where each data point belongs to the cluster with the nearest mean. The algorithm iteratively refines the

cluster centers (means) until convergence. Customer

segmentation, grouping customers based on their purchasing behavior, is a prime example.

Hierarchical Clustering:
This algorithm builds a hierarchy of clusters, representing different levels of granularity. It can be either agglomerative (bottom-up) or divisive (top-down). Analyzing gene expression data to group genes with similar expression patterns is a common application.

DBSCAN (Density-Based Spatial Clustering of
Applications with Noise):
This algorithm groups data points based on their density. It identifies clusters as dense regions separated by sparser regions. Detecting anomalies or outliers in data, such as identifying fraudulent transactions, is a suitable use case.

Reinforcement Learning Algorithms:

While not directly part of the AI-900's core focus on machine learning
algorithms, a basic understanding is beneficial.
Reinforcement learning involves an agent learning to interact with an environment to maximize a reward.

Q-Learning:

This algorithm learns a Q-function that
estimates the expected reward for taking a particular action in a given state. Training a robot to navigate a maze is a classic example.

This exploration provides a foundational understanding of key machine learning algorithms. Remember that choosing the right algorithm depends heavily on the specific problem, the type of data, and the desired outcome. The AI-900 exam focuses on understanding the capabilities and limitations of these algorithms, so practicing with different datasets and exploring

Azure's machine learning tools will significantly enhance your preparation. Don't hesitate to experiment with Azure's free tier to gain practical hands-on experience with these algorithms and solidify your understanding. The real-world examples provided throughout aim to contextualize these algorithms, making them easier to grasp and remember for the exam. Further exploration into specific algorithm parameters and advanced techniques will build a more comprehensive understanding as you progress.

Anomaly Detection Techniques and Applications

Anomaly detection, a crucial aspect of unsupervised
machine learning, focuses on identifying data points that deviate significantly from the norm. These outliers, or
anomalies, can represent errors, fraudulent activities, system failures, or simply unusual events that require further
investigation. Its significance lies in its ability to proactively uncover hidden patterns and risks, preventing potential catastrophes and improving operational efficiency across numerous domains. Understanding anomaly detection
techniques is essential for anyone preparing for the AI-900 exam, as it underscores a critical application of AI in real-world scenarios.

Several techniques are employed for anomaly detection, each with its strengths and weaknesses depending on the data's characteristics and the nature of the anomalies being sought. One common approach is statistical methods. These methods leverage statistical properties of the data to define what constitutes an anomaly. For instance, the Z-score method identifies outliers based on their distance from the mean, expressed in terms of standard deviations. Data points falling beyond a predetermined threshold (e.g., three standard deviations) are flagged as anomalies. This method is relatively simple to implement and understand, making it suitable for initial anomaly detection tasks and ideal for datasets with a normal distribution. However, its effectiveness diminishes when dealing with skewed data or complex relationships within the dataset.

Another statistical approach involves using the Interquartile Range (IQR). The IQR represents the difference between the 75th and 25th percentiles of the data. Anomalies are defined as data points falling outside a specified range determined using the IQR. This method is robust to outliers in the data itself, unlike the Z-score method which is sensitive to extreme values influencing the mean and standard deviation. The IQR approach is particularly useful when dealing with datasets containing skewed distributions or a mixture of different distributions. However, it may not be sensitive enough to detect subtle anomalies that lie within the IQR range but still represent significant deviations from typical patterns.

Moving beyond simple statistical methods, machine learning algorithms offer powerful tools for anomaly detection.
Clustering algorithms, for example, group similar data points together. Data points that do not belong to any cluster or fall into very sparsely populated clusters are often

considered anomalies. K-means clustering, a widely used algorithm, partitions data into k clusters based on their proximity to centroids. However, choosing the optimal number of clusters (k) can be challenging and requires careful consideration.

Other clustering techniques, such as DBSCAN (Density-Based Spatial Clustering of Applications with Noise), are more effective at identifying arbitrarily shaped clusters and handling noise in the data, thereby improving the accuracy of anomaly detection.

Another effective class of machine learning algorithms for anomaly detection are classification algorithms. These are primarily designed for supervised learning, but they can be adapted for anomaly detection using a technique called One-Class SVM (Support Vector Machine). One-Class SVM builds a model representing the normal data points, and any data point significantly deviating from this model is classified as an anomaly. This method excels in situations where the number

of anomalies is considerably smaller
than the number of normal data
points, a typical characteristic of

many real-world scenarios. This is because it focuses on modeling the 'normal' behavior instead of explicitly modeling the anomalies.

Neural networks, particularly autoencoders, provide another sophisticated approach. Autoencoders are designed to learn a compressed representation of the input data and then reconstruct it. Anomalies are identified by comparing the reconstructed data to the original input data. Significant discrepancies indicate potential anomalies. The advantage of autoencoders lies in their ability to learn complex, non-linear relationships within the data, making them effective at detecting subtle anomalies that might be missed by simpler methods. However, autoencoders require significant computational resources and expertise to train and optimize effectively. This makes them a more advanced choice for anomaly detection compared to simpler statistical or machine learning approaches.

The applications of anomaly detection are extensive and impactful. In fraud detection, anomaly detection algorithms analyze financial transactions to identify unusual patterns indicative of fraudulent activities such as unauthorized access, identity theft, or insurance claims fraud. By analyzing transaction amounts, frequencies, locations, and other relevant features, these algorithms can quickly flag suspicious activities for further investigation. This significantly reduces financial losses and improves the security of financial systems.

Network security benefits greatly from anomaly detection. Network intrusion detection systems use anomaly detection techniques to monitor network traffic for unusual activities that may signal cyberattacks or malware infections. Anomalies such as unusual access patterns, high data transfer rates, or connections to suspicious IP addresses are flagged as potential threats. Early detection of anomalies enables prompt responses, minimizing potential damages and safeguarding sensitive information. This is increasingly critical in today's interconnected world where cyber threats are constantly evolving.

Predictive maintenance leverages anomaly detection to predict equipment failures before they occur. By analyzing sensor data from industrial machinery, these algorithms can identify patterns that indicate impending malfunctions. Early detection enables proactive maintenance, minimizing downtime, reducing repair costs, and improving overall system reliability. This is of particular importance in industries where equipment failure can lead to significant financial losses or safety risks, such as manufacturing, aviation, and energy production.

Healthcare also benefits tremendously. Anomaly detection can analyze patient data, including vital signs, medical images, and lab results, to identify unusual patterns that may indicate potential health problems. Early detection can lead to prompt diagnosis and treatment, improving patient outcomes. This application requires careful consideration of ethical and privacy implications, emphasizing responsible AI practices.

Choosing the optimal anomaly detection technique depends on several factors: the type of data, the nature of the anomalies, the computational resources available, and the desired level of accuracy. A comprehensive approach often involves combining multiple techniques to improve the accuracy and robustness of anomaly detection. For instance, a simple statistical method might be used for initial screening, followed by a more sophisticated machine learning algorithm to investigate potentially anomalous data points flagged by the initial screening. Moreover, it's vital to

understand the limitations of each technique and to evaluate their performance using appropriate metrics such as
precision, recall, and F1-score.

The AI-900 exam assesses understanding of these core concepts and their applications. Preparing for the exam requires not only memorizing the various techniques but also understanding their underlying principles and their suitability for different applications. Hands-on experience with Azure's machine learning tools, including exploring datasets and experimenting with different algorithms, will substantially enhance your comprehension and preparedness for the exam. Remember that the focus is not only on
what the algorithms do, but crucially *why*
they are chosen for specific tasks, and their inherent limitations, mirroring

the real-world challenges faced when deploying these powerful tools. The ability to articulate these aspects demonstrates a strong grasp of the subject matter. Through consistent learning and practical application, success on the AI-900 exam becomes attainable. The resources provided in this book, alongside exploration of Azure's free tier, will empower your learning journey.

Fundamentals of Computer Vision

Computer vision, a vibrant field within artificial intelligence, empowers computers to "see" and interpret images and videos in a way analogous to human vision. It's not just about recognizing objects; it's about understanding the context, relationships, and actions within visual data. This ability has revolutionized numerous industries, from healthcare and manufacturing to autonomous vehicles and retail. At its core, computer vision involves a complex interplay of image acquisition, preprocessing, feature extraction, and pattern recognition.

Let's begin with the fundamental building blocks of computer vision. Image acquisition involves capturing the visual data, whether through a digital camera, a smartphone, or other imaging devices. The quality of this initial data significantly impacts the accuracy of subsequent analysis. Factors like resolution, lighting conditions, and noise levels all play crucial roles. Preprocessing then cleans and prepares the raw image data. This often involves steps like noise reduction, image enhancement (sharpening or contrast adjustment), and geometric transformations (resizing or rotation) to optimize the image for further processing.

Feature extraction is arguably the most critical step. It involves identifying salient features within the image that are crucial for distinguishing different objects or patterns. These features can range from simple characteristics like edges and corners to more complex representations like textures and shapes. Traditional methods involved handcrafted features, where domain experts designed algorithms to extract specific features. However, modern computer vision heavily relies on deep learning techniques, particularly convolutional neural

networks (CNNs), which
automatically learn these features
from vast amounts of training data.
CNNs excel at detecting intricate
patterns and relationships within
images, far
exceeding the capabilities of
handcrafted features.

The extracted features are then used
for pattern recognition, the process
of classifying, identifying, or
categorizing
objects or scenes in the image. This
is often achieved using machine
learning algorithms trained on large,
labeled
datasets. For instance, a system
might be trained to identify different
types of fruits by feeding it
thousands of images of apples,
bananas, oranges, etc., each labeled
with its
corresponding type. The algorithm
learns the visual features that
distinguish one type of fruit from

another, enabling it to accurately classify new, unseen images.

Several key concepts underpin the functionality of computer vision systems:

Image Classification:
This involves assigning a single label to an entire image, indicating the dominant object or scene depicted. For example, classifying an image as "cat," "dog," or "bird." Deep learning models, particularly CNNs, have achieved remarkable accuracy in this task, often exceeding human performance in certain scenarios.

Object Detection:
This goes beyond simple classification by identifying multiple objects within an image and specifying their locations using bounding boxes. This is crucial for applications like autonomous driving, where the system needs to locate pedestrians, vehicles, and traffic signs accurately. Popular object detection models include YOLO (You Only Look Once) and Faster R-CNN

(Region-based Convolutional Neural Networks).

Image Segmentation:
This is the most detailed level of analysis, dividing the image into meaningful regions based on their semantic content. Instead of just identifying the presence of an object, image segmentation precisely outlines the boundaries of each object. This is crucial for applications like medical imaging, where accurate segmentation of organs or lesions is critical for diagnosis and treatment planning. Common segmentation techniques include U-Net and Mask R-CNN.

Image Retrieval:
This involves searching for similar images within a large database based on visual similarity. This is widely used in reverse image search engines, where users can upload an image to find visually similar images online. Content-based image retrieval (CBIR) systems use feature extraction and similarity measures to find the best matches.

The applications of computer vision are incredibly diverse and continue to expand at a rapid pace. Here are just a few illustrative examples:

Healthcare:
Computer vision is used for medical image analysis, aiding in the detection of diseases like cancer, analyzing X-rays, MRIs, and CT scans. It also assists in surgical planning and robotic surgery.

Autonomous Vehicles:
Self-driving cars rely heavily on computer vision for object detection, lane recognition, and navigation. They use cameras and other sensors to perceive their surroundings and make decisions about speed, steering, and braking.

Retail:
Computer vision is used for inventory management, customer behavior analysis, and security surveillance in retail settings. It can track items on shelves, analyze

customer traffic patterns, and detect shoplifting.

Manufacturing:
Computer vision systems can inspect products for defects, guide robotic arms during assembly, and optimize production processes. They ensure quality control and increase efficiency.

Security and Surveillance:
Computer vision plays a significant role in security systems, identifying suspicious activities, facial recognition, and monitoring public spaces.

Agriculture:
Precision agriculture utilizes computer vision for crop monitoring, disease detection, and yield prediction. Drones equipped with cameras can capture images of fields, allowing farmers to assess crop health and make informed decisions.

The power of computer vision is largely driven by advancements in deep learning and the availability of massive datasets. The more data these models are trained on, the more accurate and robust they become. However, ethical considerations are paramount. Bias in training data can lead to biased outcomes, and issues of privacy need careful consideration, particularly when using computer vision for facial recognition or surveillance. Responsible development and deployment of computer vision systems are crucial to ensure fairness, accountability, and ethical use of this powerful technology.

Beyond the core concepts, the practical implementation of computer vision often involves dealing with challenges like variations in lighting, occlusion (objects partially blocking each other), and scale changes (objects appearing at different sizes). Robust computer vision systems must be able to handle these challenges effectively to maintain accuracy and

reliability. Furthermore, the
computational demands of deep

learning models can be substantial, requiring powerful hardware and efficient algorithms for real-time applications.

The field continues to evolve rapidly, with ongoing research focused on improving accuracy, efficiency, and robustness.
New architectures, training techniques, and datasets are constantly emerging, pushing the boundaries of what's
possible. The integration of computer vision with other AI technologies, such as natural language processing and
robotics, is also leading to innovative applications that are transforming various aspects of our lives. The future of computer vision is bright, promising even more exciting advancements and widespread applications across numerous domains. Understanding the fundamentals is just the starting point;

continuous learning and exploration are key to staying abreast of the latest developments in this dynamic field. The practical applications discussed here represent only a small fraction of the potential of computer vision. As the
technology continues to evolve, we can expect even more creative and impactful uses to emerge in the years to come.
The intersection of computer vision and other AI
technologies promises to unlock even greater possibilities.
For example, combining computer vision with natural
language processing could lead to systems that not only "see" but also "understand" and describe what they see, bridging the gap between visual perception and human comprehension. This interdisciplinary approach is already driving advancements in areas such as augmented reality, where computer vision overlays digital information onto the real world.

Services and Applications

Azure provides a robust suite of
cloud-based services
specifically designed to empower
developers and data
scientists to leverage the power of
computer vision. These services, built
on Microsoft's cutting-edge AI
technologies, abstract away the
complexities of building and
deploying computer vision models,
enabling rapid development and
deployment of sophisticated
applications. Let's explore three key
Azure services: the Computer Vision
service, the Face service, and the
Form Recognizer.

The Azure Computer Vision service is
a versatile and
powerful tool offering a wide range of
image analysis
capabilities. It uses deep learning

models pre-trained on massive datasets to analyze images and extract valuable insights. This service goes beyond simple object detection; it can identify objects, scenes, and even extract textual

information from images. The API is incredibly straightforward, allowing developers to integrate computer vision capabilities into their applications with minimal effort. For instance, developers can use the Computer Vision API to determine the dominant colors in an image, detect celebrities, or even analyze the overall aesthetic quality of an image—all without the need to build and train their own complex models.

Consider a scenario where you want to automatically tag images uploaded to a website for improved search functionality. Instead of manually tagging each image, you can integrate the Azure Computer Vision API. The API will analyze the image, identify objects and scenes, and automatically generate relevant tags.

This automation
drastically improves efficiency and
scalability. Further, the

API's ability to identify celebrities is valuable for applications like social media platforms or entertainment websites, allowing for automatic tagging of images featuring known personalities. The accuracy of these functionalities is continuously improved through ongoing model training and updates by Microsoft. The service also provides detailed analysis for image moderation, which is crucial for applications requiring content filtering or compliance with content guidelines.

Let's look at a simple code example using Python to analyze an image with the Computer Vision API:

```python
from azure.cognitiveservices.vision.computervision import ComputerVisionClient
from
```

```python
azure.cognitiveservices.vision.comp
utervision.models import
VisualFeatureTypes
from msrest.authentication import
CognitiveServicesCredentials
```

Replace with your subscription key and endpoint

subscription

key = *"YOUR*

SUBSCRIPTION_KEY"

endpoint =

"YOUR_ENDPOINT"

credentials =

CognitiveServicesCredentials(s

ubscription_key)

client =

ComputerVisionClient(endpoint

, credentials) image

url = *"YOUR*

IMAGE_URL"

Analyze the image

```
analysis = client.analyze
image(image
url, visual_features=
[VisualFeatureTypes.objects,
VisualFeatureTypes.tags,
VisualFeatureTypes.description])
```

Print the results

```
print("Objects detected:",
analysis.objects)
print("Tags:", analysis.tags)
print("Description:",
analysis.description.captions[0].text
)
```

```
```

Remember to replace `"YOUR SUBSCRIPTION KEY"`, `"YOUR ENDPOINT"`, and `"YOUR IMAGE_URL"` with your actual values. This code snippet demonstrates how easily you can incorporate the Computer Vision API into your applications to perform powerful image analysis tasks.
The comprehensive documentation provided by Microsoft facilitates further exploration and integration of

the advanced functionalities offered by the Computer Vision API. You can explore functionalities such as OCR (Optical Character Recognition) for extracting text from images and handwritten documents, face detection and analysis, and image similarity comparison.

The Azure Face service provides specialized capabilities for facial recognition, analysis, and identification. Unlike the broader Computer Vision service, the Face service focuses exclusively on facial features. It can detect faces within an image, analyze facial attributes such as age, gender, and emotion, and even identify individuals based on previously registered faces. This service is particularly useful for applications requiring robust facial recognition, like security systems, law enforcement, or personalized user experiences. The service is also designed with privacy considerations in mind, adhering to strict guidelines for data handling and storage.

Imagine a scenario where you're building a security system for a building. The Azure Face service could be integrated to identify authorized personnel by comparing their faces
against a database of registered faces. This creates a highly secure and efficient access control system. The service's ability to analyze facial attributes also allows for more personalized user experiences. For example, an application could tailor its recommendations or content based on the detected age and gender of a user. The Face service API also provides functionalities for detecting facial landmarks,
allowing for detailed analysis of facial expressions and head poses.
Advanced functionalities include the ability to verify if two faces belong to the same person and identify similar faces within a large dataset. However, it's imperative to utilize this service responsibly, adhering to ethical

considerations and privacy regulations.

Finally, the Azure Form Recognizer is a specialized service designed for extracting information from forms and documents. It leverages advanced AI techniques to automatically identify and extract key information from various document types, including invoices, receipts, and IDs. This service significantly reduces the manual effort required for data entry, improving efficiency and accuracy. It supports various file formats, including images (JPEG, PNG, etc.) and PDFs. The service can adapt to different layouts and styles of forms, making it highly versatile.

Let's envision an application designed for automating expense report processing. The Azure Form Recognizer can automatically extract information such as date, vendor name, amount, and description from scanned receipts. This data can then be automatically imported into accounting systems, eliminating manual data entry and reducing the potential for errors. The service also offers customization options, allowing developers to train custom models for specific form

types. This is particularly useful for organizations with
unique forms or documents. The Form Recognizer's ability to handle various languages also enhances its versatility, making it applicable for diverse applications. Microsoft continuously improves the underlying models, ensuring accurate and reliable extraction of information from complex forms and documents. The service offers detailed insights into the extraction process, highlighting confidence scores and enabling developers to fine-tune the results.

In summary, Azure's Computer Vision suite offers a
comprehensive set of services to address a wide range of computer vision tasks. The Computer Vision, Face, and Form Recognizer services provide powerful and accessible tools for building intelligent applications without requiring extensive expertise in machine learning. The ease of

integration with other Azure services further enhances their usability and effectiveness. By leveraging these services, developers can unlock the power of computer vision to create innovative and impactful applications across diverse domains. Remember to explore the extensive documentation and tutorials provided by Microsoft to unlock the full potential of these valuable tools. The continuous updates and improvements ensure that these services remain at the

forefront of computer vision technology. Understanding their capabilities is crucial for any developer or data scientist looking to integrate computer vision into their projects. Each service's specialization allows for focused and efficient solutions, thereby maximizing the impact of computer vision technologies. Responsible use and adherence to ethical

guidelines are paramount when deploying such powerful tools.

Introduction to Natural Language Processing NLP

Building upon our exploration of computer vision in Azure, we now turn our attention to another crucial area of artificial intelligence: Natural Language Processing (NLP). NLP bridges the gap between human language and computer understanding, enabling machines to process, interpret, and generate human language. This capability is fundamental to numerous applications, from chatbots and virtual assistants to machine translation and sentiment analysis. Unlike computer vision, which deals with visual data, NLP focuses on textual and spoken data, extracting meaning and insights that would otherwise be inaccessible to computers.

The core challenge in NLP lies in the inherent ambiguity and complexity of human language. Words can have multiple meanings depending on context, grammar can be nuanced and irregular, and even subtle variations in tone or phrasing can drastically alter the intended meaning. NLP techniques aim to overcome these challenges by employing a range of sophisticated algorithms and statistical models to analyze and interpret linguistic data.

One of the foundational tasks in NLP is text preprocessing. This crucial initial step involves cleaning and preparing the raw text data for further analysis. It typically includes tasks such as tokenization (breaking down text into individual words or phrases), stemming or lemmatization (reducing words to their root form), stop word removal (eliminating common words like "the," "a," and "is" that often carry little meaning), and handling punctuation and special characters. The quality of text preprocessing significantly impacts the accuracy and

effectiveness of subsequent NLP
tasks.

Consider, for instance, the sentence "The
quick brown fox

jumps over the lazy dog."
Tokenization would break it into
individual words: ["The", "quick",
"brown", "fox", "jumps", "over",
"the", "lazy", "dog"]. Stop word
removal would then remove "The"
and "the," leaving a more concise
representation for analysis.

Beyond preprocessing, several core
NLP techniques are commonly
employed. Text classification
involves assigning predefined
categories to text documents. For
example, classifying email messages
as spam or not spam, or
categorizing news articles by topic
(politics, sports,
business). This is often achieved
using machine learning algorithms
such as Naive Bayes, Support Vector
Machines (SVMs), or deep learning
models like Recurrent Neural
Networks (RNNs) and transformers.
These algorithms learn patterns and
relationships within the text data to

make accurate classifications. The training data used is critical; a well-labeled dataset of appropriately categorized text is essential for the model's success. An insufficient or biased training set will likely result in a model with low accuracy and potential for skewed outcomes.

Sentiment analysis is another crucial NLP application, focusing on determining the emotional tone expressed in text. Is the sentiment positive, negative, or neutral? This has wide-ranging applications, from analyzing customer reviews to gauging public opinion on social media. Sentiment analysis often leverages techniques like lexicon-based approaches (using dictionaries of words with associated sentiment scores) or machine learning models trained on labeled data. Consider the task of analyzing customer reviews of a new phone. A positive review might contain words like "amazing," "excellent," and "love," while a negative review might use words like

"disappointing,"
"terrible," and "hate." A sentiment
analysis model can
effectively identify these patterns and
assign overall

sentiment scores. However, the subtleties of language, such as sarcasm or irony, can pose significant challenges.

Named Entity Recognition (NER) is a technique used to identify and classify named entities in text, such as people, organizations, locations, dates, and monetary values. For example, in the sentence "Bill Gates founded Microsoft in 1975," NER would identify "Bill Gates" as a person, "Microsoft" as an organization, and "1975" as a date. NER is often used in information extraction and knowledge graph construction, allowing systems to automatically extract key information from large volumes of text. This is crucial for tasks such as building knowledge bases, creating customer relationship management (CRM) systems, and powering search engines.

Beyond these core techniques, advanced NLP capabilities include machine translation (automatically translating text from one language to another), question answering (allowing computers to answer questions posed in natural language), text summarization (generating concise summaries of longer texts), and dialogue systems (creating chatbots and virtual assistants capable of engaging in natural conversations). Each of these advanced capabilities leverages multiple NLP techniques, often combined with other AI technologies such as speech recognition and computer vision. For instance, a sophisticated chatbot might integrate speech recognition to convert spoken input into text, NLP to understand the meaning of the text, a knowledge base to access relevant information, and a text-to-speech engine to generate a spoken response.

The practical applications of NLP are vast and continuously expanding. In the business world, NLP powers customer service chatbots, automates document processing, analyzes market trends, and personalizes marketing campaigns. In healthcare, NLP assists in medical diagnosis, analyzes patient records, and speeds up drug discovery. In education, NLP can personalize learning experiences, provide automated feedback on student writing, and translate educational materials. The potential benefits are immense, but responsible development and deployment are critical.

Ethical considerations are paramount when using NLP. Bias in training data can lead to biased outputs, perpetuating stereotypes and potentially causing harm. Privacy concerns arise when processing personal data, requiring careful consideration of data security and anonymization techniques. Transparency in NLP systems is essential to understand how they make decisions and to identify potential biases.

Accountability is crucial to address any negative consequences that may arise from the use of NLP technologies. Microsoft, in line with its responsible AI principles, actively promotes the development and deployment of ethical and fair NLP systems.

Azure provides a range of cloud-based NLP services to facilitate the development of NLP applications. Azure Cognitive Services for Language offers pre-built models for various NLP tasks, including sentiment analysis, text classification, NER, and language translation. This reduces the need for extensive model training and allows developers to quickly integrate NLP capabilities into their applications. Azure also provides tools for building custom NLP models, allowing developers to tailor solutions to their specific needs. These services are designed to be easily integrated with other Azure services, creating a seamless

workflow for building and deploying sophisticated AI applications. Furthermore, these services benefit from continuous
improvements and updates, keeping them at the cutting edge of NLP technology.

In conclusion, Natural Language Processing is a dynamic and rapidly evolving field with transformative potential across a broad spectrum of applications. Understanding its core techniques and ethical implications is crucial for anyone working with or building AI systems. By leveraging the power of cloud-based services like Azure Cognitive Services for Language, developers can harness the capabilities of NLP to create innovative and impactful solutions, while adhering to the principles of responsible AI development.

The future of NLP promises even more sophisticated and nuanced capabilities, pushing the boundaries of human-computer interaction and opening up new possibilities for understanding and interacting with the world around us. The journey into NLP, however, begins with a solid understanding of its core principles and a commitment to ethical development and deployment. This chapter has laid the groundwork for that understanding, preparing you to delve deeper into specific Azure services and their practical applications.

Text Analytics LUIS Speech and Translator

Azure offers a comprehensive suite of NLP services within its Cognitive Services portfolio, empowering developers to build intelligent applications capable of understanding, interpreting, and generating human language. Let's delve into four key services: Text Analytics, Language Understanding (LUIS), Speech, and Translator. Each offers unique capabilities, collectively providing a robust toolkit for various NLP tasks.

Azure Text Analytics:
This service is your go-to for extracting valuable insights from unstructured text data. It offers a range of functionalities, including sentiment analysis, key phrase extraction,

language detection, and named entity recognition (NER). Sentiment analysis gauges the overall emotional tone of a text, classifying it as positive, negative, or neutral. This is invaluable for understanding customer feedback, social media sentiment, or gauging public opinion on a particular topic. For example, analyzing customer reviews for a new product can reveal areas needing improvement based on the prevalent sentiment expressed. A negative sentiment associated with a particular feature suggests a need for redesign or improvement.

Key phrase extraction identifies the most important concepts within a text. This is particularly useful for summarizing lengthy documents or creating concise metadata. Imagine processing hundreds of news articles; key phrase extraction could automatically identify the core topics discussed, facilitating efficient information retrieval and categorization. Similarly, extracting keywords from research papers can streamline literature reviews and accelerate research progress.

Language detection automatically identifies the language of a given text, which is crucial for applications dealing with multilingual content. This allows for appropriate processing and translation, ensuring accurate and meaningful results. Consider a global e-commerce platform receiving customer inquiries in various languages. Automatic language detection prevents misinterpretations and allows for routing inquiries to the appropriate support teams.

Named entity recognition (NER) pinpoints and classifies named entities like people, organizations, locations, and dates. This can help structure unstructured data and extract relevant information for various tasks. For instance,
analyzing news articles to identify all the companies
mentioned, their locations, and associated dates provides valuable

insights for market analysis and trend identification.
Similarly, in legal document processing, NER can automatically extract relevant entities, streamlining document review and analysis.

To utilize Azure Text Analytics, you interact with its REST APIs or SDKs (Software Development Kits) in various programming languages such as Python, C, Java, etc. You simply send the text to be analyzed as input, and the service returns structured JSON outputs containing the results. For example, using the Python SDK, you might write a concise script to analyze customer feedback:

```python
from azure.ai.textanalytics import TextAnalyticsClient from azure.core.credentials import AzureKeyCredential
```

Replace with your key and endpoint

```
key = "YOUR
TEXT
ANALYTICS_KEY"
endpoint = "YOUR
TEXT
ANALYTICS_ENDPOINT"

credential =
AzureKeyCredential(key)
client =
TextAnalyticsClient(endp
oint=endpoint,
credential=credential)

documents = [
"This is a
positive
review!",
"I'm very
```

```
unhappy with
the service.",
"The product
is okay."
]

result =
client.analyze_sentiment(documents=documen
ts)

for document in result:
print(f"Document Sentiment:
{document.sentiment}")
print(f"Positive Score:
{document.confidence_scores.p
ositive}")
print(f"Negative Score:
{document.confidence_scores.n
egative}")
print(f"Neutral Score:
{document.confidence_scores.n
eutral}")
print("-" 20)

```
```

Remember to replace `"YOUR
TEXT
ANALYTICS
KEY"` *and* `"YOUR
```

TEXT
ANALYTICS
ENDPOINT"` with your actual
credentials obtained from the Azure
portal. This code

snippet showcases the simplicity and power of the Text Analytics API.

Azure Language Understanding (LUIS):
LUIS is a powerful service for building custom conversational AI models. Unlike Text Analytics, which focuses on general text analysis, LUIS specializes in understanding the intent and entities within user utterances. This is crucial for building chatbots, virtual assistants, and other applications requiring natural language interaction.

Imagine building a chatbot for an e-commerce website. Users might ask, "Show me red shoes size 8," or "I want to buy a pair of black boots." LUIS can analyze these utterances and identify the user's intent (to buy shoes or boots) and the relevant entities (color, size, type). This information is then used by the chatbot to provide appropriate responses or actions, like displaying relevant products.

Training a LUIS model involves providing example utterances and labeling their intents and entities. LUIS uses machine learning to learn the relationships between the utterances and their labels. The more training data you provide, the more accurate and robust your model becomes. LUIS provides a user-friendly interface for training and managing your models, allowing even non-programmers to build effective conversational AI applications. Furthermore, LUIS integrates seamlessly with other Azure services like the Bot Framework, simplifying the development of sophisticated chatbots.

Azure Speech service:
This service focuses on speech-to-text and text-to-speech conversion. Speech-to-text converts spoken language into written text, enabling

applications to process voice commands or transcribe audio recordings.

Text-to-speech converts written text into spoken language, powering voice assistants, audio books, and accessibility features.

Consider a transcription service for legal proceedings. The Azure Speech service can accurately transcribe the audio recordings, providing a searchable text version for efficient review and analysis. Similarly, a virtual assistant can use text-to-speech to respond to user queries in a natural and engaging way. The service supports multiple languages, making it highly versatile for applications catering to diverse audiences.

The Speech service offers customizable features, allowing developers to fine-tune models for specific accents,
vocabulary, or noise levels. This level of customization is essential for optimal performance in diverse real-world scenarios. You can access the

service through REST APIs or client SDKs, providing flexibility in integration with
different development environments. For instance, you can use the Python SDK to transcribe audio:

```python
from azure.cognitiveservices.speech import SpeechConfig,
AudioConfig, SpeechRecognizer
```

Replace with your key and region

```
speech
key = "YOUR
SPEECH_KEY"
speech
region = "YOUR
SPEECH_REGION"

speech
config =
SpeechConfig(subscription=speec
h
key, region=speech_region)
audio_config =
AudioConfig(filename="audio.wa
v") Replace with your audio file
speech
recognizer =
SpeechRecognizer(speech
config, audio_config)
```

```python
result = speech
recognizer.recognize
once_async().get()

if result.reason ==
speechsdk.ResultReason.Recogniz
edSpeech:
print(f"Recognized: {result.text}")
elif result.reason ==
speechsdk.ResultReason.NoMatch
: print("No speech could be
recognized")
elif result.reason ==
speechsdk.ResultReason.Canceled
: cancellation
details = result.cancellation
details
print(f"Speech recognition
canceled:
{cancellation_details.reason}")
if cancellation_details.reason ==
speechsdk.CancellationReason.Err
or:
print(f"Error details: {cancellation
details.error
details}") ```
```

Again, remember to replace `"YOUR
SPEECH
KEY"` and `"YOUR

*SPEECH
REGION"`* with your Azure
credentials.
This example showcases the basic
transcription
functionality; more advanced
features are readily available.

Azure Translator:
This service facilitates real-time and batch translation of text between numerous languages. It leverages deep learning models to provide high-quality, accurate translations. It's ideal for applications requiring multilingual support, such as websites, mobile apps, or customer support systems.

Imagine an international e-commerce platform. Azure Translator can automatically translate product descriptions, customer reviews, and support articles into various languages, ensuring accessibility for a global customer base.
It also supports various translation modes, including text translation, document translation, and even speech translation. This versatility makes it a powerful tool for bridging language barriers. Similar to other services, you

can access Azure Translator via REST APIs and SDKs,
providing seamless integration into your existing
applications.

This chapter has provided a comprehensive overview of Azure's core NLP services. These services collectively represent a powerful arsenal for tackling diverse NLP challenges. By combining these services, developers can build sophisticated applications capable of understanding, interpreting, and generating human language with precision and efficiency. The key to effectively using these services lies in understanding their individual strengths and choosing the right tool for the task at hand. Remember that practical experience is invaluable; experiment with these services using Azure's free tier to solidify your understanding and build your practical skills. The possibilities for creating innovative and impactful applications using Azure's NLP capabilities are vast and continually expanding.

Building Simple NLP Applications with Azure Services

Building even the simplest NLP applications can seem daunting, but Azure's services significantly lower the barrier to entry. This section provides practical, step-by-step guides to building basic applications, focusing on ease of use and hands-on implementation. We'll leverage the services
introduced earlier – Text Analytics, LUIS, Speech, and Translator – to illustrate how readily these powerful tools can be integrated into your projects.

Let's begin with a common task: sentiment analysis. We'll use Azure's Text Analytics API to determine the overall sentiment (positive, negative, or neutral) expressed in a piece of text. This is incredibly useful for understanding customer feedback, monitoring social media conversations, or gauging public opinion on a particular topic.

First, you'll need an Azure subscription. If you don't already have one, you can sign up for a free trial. Once you have an account, navigate to the Azure portal and create a Text Analytics resource. This involves choosing a resource group, providing a name for your resource, selecting a pricing tier (the free tier is excellent for learning and experimentation), and specifying a region. The process is straightforward and guided by the Azure portal's intuitive interface.

After your Text Analytics resource is deployed (this usually takes a few minutes), you'll need to obtain its endpoint and key. These credentials are essential for authenticating your application with the service. You can find them in the resource's Overview section.

Next, we'll build a simple Python application using the `azure-ai-textanalytics` library. This library provides a convenient wrapper for interacting with the Text Analytics API. You can install it using pip: `pip install azure-ai-textanalytics`.

Here's a basic Python script that performs sentiment analysis:

```python
from azure.ai.textanalytics import TextAnalyticsClient from azure.core.credentials import AzureKeyCredential
```

Replace with your endpoint and key

```
endpoint = "YOUR
TEXT
ANALYTICS_ENDPOINT"
key = "YOUR
TEXT
ANALYTICS_KEY"

credential =
AzureKeyCredential(key)
client =
TextAnalyticsClient(endp
oint=endpoint,
credential=credential)

documents = [
"This is a fantastic
product!",
"I'm extremely
disappointed with the
service.", "The product
is okay, nothing
```

```
special."
]

result =
client.analyze_sentiment(documents=documen
ts)

for document in result:
print(f"Document:
{document.text}")
print(f"Sentiment:
{document.sentiment}")
print(f"Confidence Scores:
Positive={document.confidence
scores.positive:.2f},
Negative={document.confidence
scores.negative:.2f}, Neutral=
{document.confidence_scores.neutra
l:.2f}")
print("-" 20)
```

Remember to replace `"YOUR
TEXT
ANALYTICS
ENDPOINT"` and `"YOUR
TEXT
ANALYTICS
KEY"` with your actual endpoint and
key. This script sends a list of

documents to the Text Analytics API and receives detailed sentiment analysis for each, including confidence scores for positive, negative, and neutral sentiments. The output clearly shows the sentiment and its associated confidence level, offering a robust understanding of the expressed emotion. This simple example showcases the ease with which you can integrate powerful NLP capabilities into your applications.

Let's move on to a more sophisticated application: intent recognition with LUIS. LUIS (Language Understanding Intelligent Service) is a powerful tool for building conversational AI applications. It allows you to define intents – what the user wants to accomplish – and entities –the specific information needed to fulfill the intent.

Imagine building a simple pizza ordering bot. The intent could be "OrderPizza," and the entities might include "size," "crust," and "toppings." You would train LUIS to recognize these intents and entities from user input. This involves providing numerous example utterances for each intent, covering a range of ways a user might express their desire to order a pizza.

Creating a LUIS app is done through the LUIS portal. You'll define your intents and entities, provide example utterances, and then train your model. LUIS uses machine learning to learn the relationships between utterances and intents/entities, becoming increasingly accurate as you provide more training data.

After training, you'll obtain an endpoint and key, similar to the Text Analytics API. You can then integrate LUIS into your application to understand user intent. This integration might involve making HTTP requests to the LUIS endpoint, sending the user's input, and receiving the predicted intent and entities.

Consider a Python script interacting with LUIS:

```python
import requests
```

Replace with your LUIS endpoint and key

```
luis
endpoint = "YOUR
LUIS_ENDPOINT"
luis
key = "YOUR
LUIS_KEY"

utterance = "I want a large pepperoni pizza
with thin crust."

headers = {
"Ocp-Apim-
Subscription-Key":
luis_key, "Content-
Type":
"application/json"
}
```

```
data

=

{

"query": utterance

}
```

```python
response =
requests.post(luis_endpoint,
headers=headers, json=data)
response_json = response.json()

intent =
response_json["prediction"
]["topIntent"] entities =
response_json["prediction"
]["entities"]

print
(f"In
tent:
{inte
nt}")
print
(f"E
ntiti
es:
{enti
ties}
")
```

This script sends the user's utterance
to LUIS and receives the predicted
intent and entities. This information
can then be used to process the order,
demonstrating the power of LUIS in

understanding natural language input.
Remember to

replace placeholders with your
actual LUIS endpoint and key.

Now let's explore how to use the
Azure Speech service. This service
allows you to convert speech to text
(speech-to-text) and text to speech
(text-to-speech). This is invaluable for
building voice-enabled applications.
The process is similar to the previous
services: you create a resource in the
Azure portal, obtain the endpoint and
key, and then use the
appropriate SDK (e.g., the `azure-
cognitiveservices-speech` Python
library) to interact with the service.

For speech-to-text, you'll send an
audio stream to the service, and it will
return a transcription. For text-to-
speech, you'll provide text, and it will
generate an audio stream.

Finally, the Azure Translator service
empowers you to build applications
that translate text between multiple

languages. Again, the process involves creating a resource, obtaining credentials, and using the provided SDK. This service is particularly useful for building globally accessible applications. You can seamlessly translate user input or output, fostering cross-linguistic communication.

These examples highlight the ease with which you can integrate Azure's cognitive services into your applications.
By combining these services, you can create sophisticated NLP applications capable of performing sentiment analysis, intent recognition, speech-to-text and text-to-speech conversion, and language translation – all with minimal code and considerable power. Remember to experiment with these services using Azure's free tier to gain hands-on experience and build your expertise. The possibilities are vast; the only limit is your imagination. Through careful planning and understanding of each service's strengths, you can

create remarkably intuitive and user-friendly applications that leverage the full potential of natural language processing.

Don't be afraid to explore, experiment, and discover the numerous ways Azure's NLP services can help you solve real-world problems and create innovative solutions. The resources available in the Azure documentation are extensive and will further aid your learning journey. Consistent practice and a willingness to experiment are key to mastering these powerful tools and unlocking their full potential in your applications.

Introduction to Conversational AI

Conversational AI represents a significant leap forward in human-computer interaction, moving beyond simple command-line interfaces and static websites to create dynamic, engaging, and personalized experiences. At its core, conversational AI aims to mimic human conversation, allowing users to interact with computers using natural language – the way we communicate with each other every day. This interaction is facilitated by sophisticated algorithms and technologies that enable computers to understand, interpret, and respond to human language in a meaningful and contextually relevant way.

The applications of conversational AI are vast and rapidly expanding. We see them in everyday life, from virtual assistants like Siri and Alexa managing our schedules and answering questions, to customer service chatbots resolving issues on company websites, to sophisticated AI companions providing companionship and support. In healthcare, conversational AI powers systems that provide medical advice and monitor patient conditions. In education, it's used to create personalized learning experiences and provide instant feedback to students. In finance, it assists with managing accounts and providing financial advice. The possibilities are truly limitless, and as the technology continues to evolve, we can expect to see even more innovative applications emerge.

One of the key elements driving the success of conversational AI is natural language processing (NLP). NLP is a branch of artificial intelligence that focuses on enabling computers to understand, interpret, and generate human language. This involves tasks such as text analysis, sentiment analysis, named entity recognition, and language translation. In the context of conversational AI, NLP is crucial for enabling chatbots to understand the user's intent, extract key information from their messages, and generate appropriate responses.

Different approaches exist to building conversational AI systems. One common approach utilizes rule-based systems, where the chatbot's responses are pre-programmed based on specific keywords or phrases. This approach is simple to implement but has limitations in handling complex or unexpected inputs. A more sophisticated approach employs machine learning techniques, particularly deep learning, to train models on large datasets of conversational data. These models learn to identify patterns and generate responses that are more natural and contextually relevant than those

generated by rule-based systems.
Hybrid approaches
combine rule-based and machine
learning techniques,
leveraging the strengths of both
approaches to build more robust and
adaptable conversational AI systems.

The architecture of a conversational
AI system typically includes several
key components. A natural language
understanding (NLU) component is
responsible for
processing the user's input and
determining its intent. A dialogue
management component manages the
flow of
conversation, tracking the context and
guiding the
interaction. A natural language
generation (NLG) component
generates the chatbot's response based
on the user's intent and the current
context. These components often
interact with knowledge bases or
databases to retrieve relevant
information and provide accurate
answers to user queries.
Furthermore, sophisticated
systems may incorporate

machine learning models for tasks such as sentiment analysis, emotion detection, and personalization.

Designing effective conversational AI experiences requires careful consideration of several factors. The user interface should be intuitive and easy to navigate. The chatbot's responses should be clear, concise, and natural-sounding. The system should be able to handle unexpected inputs and gracefully recover from errors. It's crucial to incorporate mechanisms for user feedback and continuously improve the system based on user interactions. Ultimately, the goal is to create a conversational AI system that is both helpful and enjoyable to use.

The design process often begins with clearly defining the chatbot's purpose and intended audience. What specific tasks should the chatbot be able to perform? What kind of language and tone should it use? Understanding these aspects is crucial in determining the appropriate architecture and

technologies. The development process involves
iterative design and testing, with continuous feedback
incorporated to enhance the chatbot's performance and user experience. This iterative approach allows developers to refine the system's capabilities, addressing potential issues and improving its overall effectiveness.

Consider a customer service chatbot designed for a
telecommunications company. The chatbot's purpose would be to quickly and efficiently address common customer issues, such as billing inquiries, technical support requests, and account management. The target audience would be customers of varying technical expertise, requiring the
chatbot to use clear and simple language. The development process would involve designing conversation flows to guide users through common scenarios, and training machine learning models to accurately

recognize user intent and generate appropriate responses.

Another crucial aspect is the
integration of various AI
services to enhance functionality. For
example, a chatbot might integrate
with a speech-to-text service to allow
users to interact using voice
commands. It might also integrate
with a natural language understanding
service to analyze the sentiment of
user messages and tailor responses
accordingly.
Furthermore, integration with
external databases or
knowledge bases allows the chatbot
to access and retrieve relevant
information, enabling it to provide
accurate and comprehensive
answers to user queries.

Responsible AI principles are
paramount in developing
conversational AI systems. Bias in
training data can lead to biased or
unfair outcomes, and it's critical to
ensure that the chatbot's responses
are not discriminatory or offensive.

Transparency is essential – users should understand how the chatbot works and what data it collects. Privacy concerns must be addressed, and user data should be protected in accordance with relevant regulations and ethical standards.

Continuous monitoring and evaluation are necessary to identify and address any potential issues that may arise.

In conclusion, conversational AI is a powerful technology with the potential to revolutionize human-computer interaction. Its applications span numerous industries, offering opportunities to enhance efficiency, productivity, and user experience. However, it's vital to approach its development responsibly, considering ethical implications and implementing appropriate safeguards to ensure that these systems are used for good and benefit society. As the technology continues to evolve, we can anticipate increasingly sophisticated and impactful applications in various aspects of our lives. The responsible and ethical development of conversational AI is crucial to harnessing its full potential while mitigating potential risks. The focus should always be on creating systems that are helpful, engaging, and beneficial for users, while respecting their privacy and rights. This requires careful consideration of design, development, deployment, and ongoing monitoring, ensuring alignment with the principles of responsible AI.

Only through a commitment to these principles can we ensure that conversational AI systems contribute positively to society and improve the lives of users worldwide.

Azure Bot Service and Bot Framework Composer

Building upon the foundational concepts of conversational AI, we now delve into the practical implementation of these ideas within the Microsoft Azure ecosystem. Azure offers a robust suite of services specifically designed to facilitate the creation and deployment of sophisticated conversational AI applications. Central to this ecosystem are two key components: the Azure Bot Service and the Bot Framework Composer. These tools work synergistically, providing a comprehensive solution for developers of all skill levels, from seasoned professionals to those new to the field.

The Azure Bot Service acts as the backbone of your

conversational AI solution. It's a cloud-based service that manages the infrastructure required to host, scale, and manage your bots. Think of it as the engine room of your bot, handling the complexities of communication routing, message delivery, and user authentication. This allows developers to focus on the core logic and conversational flow of their bot, without needing to be deeply involved in the intricacies of server management, database interactions, or scaling infrastructure. Azure Bot Service handles these aspects seamlessly, offering automatic scaling based on demand, ensuring your bot remains responsive even during peak usage periods. This scalability is crucial, as the popularity of your bot grows, potentially requiring handling thousands of concurrent conversations. The service integrates seamlessly with other Azure services, such as Azure Cognitive Services, enabling effortless integration with advanced AI capabilities, allowing you to leverage the power of speech recognition, language understanding, and other sophisticated AI features. Furthermore, the Azure Bot Service offers robust security features, including authentication and authorization mechanisms, ensuring the confidentiality and integrity of your user data and bot interactions.

The Bot Framework Composer, on the other hand, serves as the development environment for creating and managing the conversational flow of your bot. It's a visual, low-code tool designed to empower developers of all skill levels to design engaging and effective conversational experiences. Unlike traditional coding approaches that require extensive knowledge of programming languages and frameworks, the Bot Framework Composer provides a drag-and-drop interface, making it significantly easier to construct complex conversational flows. This visual approach allows for intuitive design, reducing development time and complexity. The Composer enables developers to define the conversational paths, dialogue turns, and user interactions using a graphical representation, removing much of the tedium associated with traditional coding. This visual workflow enables rapid prototyping and iteration, allowing developers to quickly test and refine their bot's conversational capabilities.

The core strength of Bot Framework Composer lies in its ability to handle diverse conversational scenarios. You can define multiple intents (what the user wants to achieve), entities (specific pieces of information within the user's input), and dialogs (the conversation path) within the Composer's intuitive interface. Imagine building a bot for customer support. You would define intents like "request *refund*," *"check* order *status," and "ask* about_shipping." Entities might include order numbers, product names, or dates. The Composer allows you to create conversational flows that effectively handle these various intents and extract relevant entities, guiding the user through the conversation to resolve their queries efficiently. Furthermore, you can incorporate different dialogue turns, creating branching conversations based on user input, enabling a dynamic and personalized interaction. This flexibility allows for creating sophisticated conversational bots that can manage a wide range of user requests and scenarios.

The integration between the Azure Bot Service and Bot Framework Composer is seamless. Once you have designed and refined your conversational flow in the Composer, you can easily deploy it to the Azure Bot Service with a few clicks. This deployment process is straightforward and automated, eliminating manual configuration and deployment steps. This simplifies the deployment process, ensuring a smooth transition from development to production. The Azure Bot Service then manages the execution of your bot, handling communication, scaling, and security. This collaborative workflow empowers developers to focus on the creative aspects of bot development without worrying about the underlying infrastructure.

Let's consider a practical example. Suppose you are building a simple appointment scheduling bot. Using Bot Framework Composer, you would define the key intents: "schedule *appointment," "cancel* appointment," and "view_appointments." Entities would include date, time, service type, and client information. You would then create dialogs that guide the user through the process, prompting them for necessary information and validating their input.
The dialog would use conditional logic, branching the conversation based on user responses. For instance, if the user selects a particular date and time, the bot would check availability and confirm the appointment. If the chosen slot is

unavailable, the bot would prompt the user to select alternative options. This sophisticated logic is made considerably simpler through the visual interface of Bot Framework Composer.

Once complete, deploying this bot to Azure Bot Service is a straightforward process. The Composer provides a direct link to deploy to the Azure Bot Service, requiring only minimal configuration. After deployment, Azure Bot Service handles the ongoing operation of your bot, automatically scaling to handle variations in traffic. This ensures optimal performance and reliability. Further enhancements can involve integrating with other Azure Cognitive Services. For example, you might integrate with the Speech service to allow users to interact with your bot using voice commands rather than text input. You can also integrate with the Language Understanding service (LUIS) for more nuanced natural language processing capabilities, allowing your bot to better understand user intent even with ambiguous or imprecise phrasing. This integration provides a richer and more intuitive user experience, expanding the functionality of your bot considerably.

The Azure Bot Service also provides valuable monitoring and analytics capabilities. Through the Azure portal, you can track key metrics, such as conversation volume, successful interactions, and error rates. This data provides insights into your bot's performance and areas for improvement. You can track popular conversational paths, identify areas where users struggle, and monitor error rates to ensure smooth operation. These insights are crucial for continuous improvement, allowing you to iterate and refine your bot's performance based on real-world usage data. This iterative process is key to creating a successful conversational AI application.

Beyond the core functionalities, Azure Bot Service integrates well with various channels, allowing you to deploy your bot across multiple platforms.

This means your bot can be
accessible through popular
messaging

applications such as Microsoft Teams, Facebook Messenger, Slack, and more. This multi-channel support broadens the reach of your bot, allowing it to engage with a wider audience across their preferred communication channels. Expanding the accessibility of your bot is crucial in maximizing its potential reach and impact.

In conclusion, the combination of the Azure Bot Service and Bot Framework Composer presents a powerful and accessible platform for building and deploying sophisticated conversational AI applications. The low-code approach of the Composer empowers developers of all skill levels to create rich and engaging conversational experiences, while the robust infrastructure and scalability of the Azure Bot Service ensures reliable operation and efficient scaling to meet changing demand. The integration with other Azure services further enhances the capabilities of your bot, allowing for the incorporation of advanced AI features and seamless deployment across multiple channels. The ability to monitor and analyze performance data is also crucial for iterative improvement, ensuring your bot remains relevant and effective over time. Mastering these tools is crucial for any aspiring AI professional seeking to leverage the power of conversational AI. Using the free tier of Azure provides an excellent hands-on opportunity to experiment and build your skills, paving the way for creating impactful and user-friendly conversational AI applications.

Building a Simple Chatbot with the Azure Bot Service

Building even a rudimentary chatbot using the Azure Bot Service is surprisingly straightforward. The service abstracts away much of the underlying complexity, allowing developers to focus on the conversational logic rather than low-level infrastructure management. We'll walk through creating a simple chatbot that responds to a few predefined keywords. This example will utilize the Bot Framework Composer, a visual tool that simplifies the bot-building process. Before we start, ensure you have an active Azure subscription and familiarity with the Azure portal. The free tier is perfectly adequate for this exercise.

Our first step involves creating a new bot resource in Azure. Navigate to the

Azure portal (portal.azure.com) and search for "Bot Service." Click on "Create" to initiate the bot creation process. You'll need to provide a resource group (create a new one if you don't have one), a globally unique bot name, a pricing tier (again, the free tier is suitable for our learning purposes), and select a region geographically closest to your location for optimal performance and latency.

You'll also need to specify an app service plan, which dictates the resource allocation for your bot. Choosing the appropriate App Service Plan depends on several factors, including anticipated traffic and the complexity of your bot. For a simple chatbot like ours, a smaller plan should suffice. Remember to note the resource group and bot name as you'll need this information later. After completing these steps, click "Review + create" to provision your bot in Azure. This process might take a few minutes.

Once the bot resource is successfully created, you'll find the resource overview page within the Azure portal. Crucially, you'll find the "Channels" section. Channels represent the various ways users can interact with your bot. Popular choices include web chat, Microsoft Teams, Facebook Messenger, and more. For this example, we'll focus on web chat, the simplest way to test and interact with our chatbot directly from the browser. Select "Web Chat" and configure the channel appropriately. Azure will provide you with the necessary configuration details and keys, essential for connecting your chatbot to the selected channel.

Now, let's turn our attention to the Bot Framework
Composer, the tool we'll use to design the conversational flow of our chatbot. Download and install the Composer from the official Microsoft

website. Upon launching the Composer, you'll be prompted to create a new bot project. You can choose between creating a new bot from scratch or using a pre-built template. For our simple chatbot, starting from scratch is the most instructive. You'll be asked to provide a name for your bot project, and most importantly, you'll need to select the language you wish to program in (popular options include C and JavaScript). C offers a bit more structured programming experience, while JavaScript might be preferred for a faster development process, depending on your programming background. Select the language that suits your comfort level best, as the underlying principles remain consistent across these languages.

Next, we need to connect the Composer to our Azure bot resource. This involves providing the relevant information from our Azure portal, including the bot name and the associated keys. These keys provide secure access to your bot resource, authorizing the Composer to make changes and deploy updates to your bot. The exact steps to connect are clearly shown within the Composer interface; follow the instructions carefully to ensure a seamless connection.

The core of bot development lies in defining the conversational dialog. The Bot Framework Composer uses a visual dialog management system, allowing you to represent the conversational flow using nodes and arrows. This approach makes it intuitive to design even complex conversations. For our simple chatbot, we'll create a few simple dialogs that handle basic greetings and respond to specific keywords. We'll start with a "Welcome" dialog, triggered when a user initiates the conversation. Within this dialog, we can add a simple greeting message such as, "Hello! How can I help you today?".

Now, let's create a few more dialogs to handle specific user inputs. We'll

implement a dialog to respond to the keyword "weather." In this dialog, we could integrate with a weather API (a service that provides weather data) to give the user up-to-date information on the current weather. The Composer facilitates this integration by allowing you to add custom code and interact with external services. However, for simplicity's sake, let's create a simpler response such as "The weather is currently unavailable, please try again later".
This demonstrates how to incorporate external API interaction later if desired.

Similarly, we can create dialogs to respond to other keywords, such as "time," providing the current time, or "help," presenting a menu of available commands or options.
Each dialog will have an input trigger (the keyword), a simple processing step (possibly incorporating an external API), and an output response (the answer to the user's query).

Remember to test your bot frequently throughout the
development process. The Composer allows you to test the chatbot directly within the tool, simulating user interactions. This iterative testing is crucial for identifying and correcting errors or ambiguities in your dialog flow.

Once you're satisfied with your chatbot's responses and conversational flow, you can deploy it to Azure. The Composer simplifies this process, allowing you to publish your bot directly from within the application. Upon
deployment, Azure will take care of hosting and scaling your chatbot based on the resource allocation you specified during the bot resource creation. Deploying the bot essentially pushes all the changes to the live Azure bot resource, making it immediately accessible via the chosen channels.

After deployment, your simple chatbot is ready to be used. Access it through the web chat channel using the URL provided by Azure. You can experiment with different user inputs, testing each dialog you've created. Observe the interaction, verifying that your bot responds as expected to various queries and commands.

This simple chatbot provides a fundamental understanding of how to use the Azure Bot Service and Bot Framework Composer. This foundation enables you to construct increasingly sophisticated conversational AI applications. While this example focused on a few simple keywords and responses, the potential to add more complex functionalities, such as natural language understanding (NLU), dialogue management, and integration with other Azure services (Cognitive Services, for example), is boundless.

The next step in improving this chatbot might involve integrating

Azure Cognitive Services. For example, integrating the Language Understanding service (LUIS) would enable the bot to understand more natural language inputs rather than just specific keywords. LUIS allows you to train a model to recognize user intent even if the wording is slightly different, making the bot much more robust and user-friendly. Similarly, integrating the QnA Maker service would allow you to create a knowledge base of frequently asked questions, enabling the bot to respond to a wider range of inquiries. These additions drastically increase the chatbot's intelligence and conversational capabilities. Remember to use the Azure free tier to explore these integrations without incurring immediate costs; it allows hands-on learning with minimal financial commitment. This step-by-step guide showcases how to build, test, deploy, and enhance a basic chatbot using Azure services. This lays a strong foundation for further exploration of more advanced conversational AI techniques within the Azure environment.

Remember, the key to building successful chatbots lies in iterative development, continuous testing, and refinement based on user feedback.

Integrating AI Services into Chatbots

Building upon the foundation of a
basic chatbot created with the Azure
Bot Service and Bot Framework
Composer, we now explore the
significant enhancements achievable
by integrating other Azure Cognitive
Services. This integration transforms a
simple keyword-based bot into a
sophisticated conversational AI
capable of understanding natural
language, recognizing speech, and
responding in a far more human-like
manner. Let's delve into how we can
seamlessly integrate services like
LUIS (Language Understanding
Intelligent Service) and the Speech
service to unlock this enhanced
functionality.

The limitations of a keyword-based
chatbot are immediately apparent. Its
understanding is brittle; even a slight

variation in phrasing can lead to a failure to recognize the user's intent. This is where LUIS shines. LUIS acts as the brain of our chatbot, allowing it to interpret the meaning behind natural language input. Instead of relying on exact keyword matches, LUIS uses machine learning to understand the intent behind the user's message, regardless of the specific words used.

To integrate LUIS, we first need to create a LUIS app. This involves defining the intents (what the user wants to achieve) and entities (key pieces of information within the user's utterance). For example, if our chatbot is designed to help users book appointments, we might define intents such as "BookAppointment," "CancelAppointment," and "CheckAvailability." Entities could include "date," "time," "serviceType," and "location." We then train the LUIS model by providing example utterances for each intent and annotating the entities within those utterances. The more varied and comprehensive our training data, the more accurate and robust our LUIS model will be.

Once the LUIS model is trained and published, we can access it from within the Bot Framework Composer. This typically involves adding a LUIS recognizer to our bot's dialog. The recognizer will send the user's input to the LUIS endpoint, receive the predicted intent and entities, and use this information to trigger the appropriate response within the bot's logic. This allows the bot to handle a wide range of user inputs that express the same underlying intent, significantly improving its conversational capabilities. For instance, a user might say "I want to book a haircut next Tuesday at 3 pm," or "Schedule a haircut for Tuesday afternoon," or even "Get me a haircut appointment next Tuesday." All of these express the same intent

("BookAppointment") but would fail with a keyword-based system. With LUIS, the bot will correctly interpret each of these variations.

Effective utilization of LUIS requires careful consideration of the training data. It's crucial to account for variations in language, slang, misspellings, and different ways of expressing the same intent. Regularly evaluating and
retraining the model is essential to maintain accuracy and adapt to changes in user language. Microsoft provides
extensive documentation and tools to monitor the
performance of your LUIS app, allowing you to identify areas for improvement and refine your model over time. This iterative process ensures that your chatbot continues to understand user input with high accuracy.

Beyond understanding natural language, enhancing the user experience often involves incorporating speech capabilities.

Azure's Speech service offers powerful tools for converting spoken language into text (speech-to-text) and generating

synthesized speech from text (text-to-speech). This
integration allows users to interact with the chatbot through voice commands, making the experience more natural and accessible.

Integrating the Speech service into our chatbot within the Bot Framework Composer is similar to integrating LUIS. We would add a speech recognizer to our bot's dialog, which would send the audio input to the Speech service for
transcription. The transcribed text would then be processed by LUIS or other parts of our bot's logic to determine the user's intent. Similarly, when the bot needs to respond, we would use the text-to-speech functionality of the Speech service to generate audio output. This bidirectional audio integration provides a significant leap forward in conversational AI, creating a more intuitive and user-friendly interaction.

However, integrating speech presents additional challenges. Considerations such as background noise, accents, and variations in speech patterns can impact the accuracy of speech-to-text conversion. Choosing the appropriate Speech service language model and optimizing audio input quality are crucial steps to ensure accurate transcription. Regular testing with real-world users under various conditions is essential to identify areas needing improvement. Furthermore, the text-to-speech feature needs to be carefully configured to produce clear, natural-sounding speech. Experimenting with different voices and settings is advisable to achieve the best user experience.

While LUIS and the Speech service enhance the chatbot significantly, their effective integration demands careful planning and iterative development. Consider the following:

Intent and Entity Design:
Thoroughly define the intents and entities in your LUIS app to accurately capture the scope of user interactions. Avoid overly broad or ambiguous
intents, and ensure entities are clearly defined to extract meaningful information from user utterances. Start small, focusing on a core set of functionalities, and gradually expand as needed.

Error Handling:
Implement robust error handling to gracefully handle situations where LUIS fails to recognize the intent or the Speech service encounters transcription errors. This could involve providing fallback responses or prompting the user for clarification.

Context Management:
Maintain context throughout the conversation. The chatbot should

remember previous interactions and utilize this information to provide relevant responses. This requires careful design of the conversational flow and efficient storage of conversation history.

Deployment and Monitoring:
Deploy the chatbot to a suitable environment, whether it's a testing environment or a production environment. Continuously monitor its
performance and gather user feedback to identify areas for improvement and refine your models. Utilize Azure's monitoring tools to track metrics such as response time, accuracy, and error rates.

Security and Privacy:
Adhere to best practices for security and data privacy. Ensure that user data is handled
responsibly and in compliance with relevant regulations. Consider encrypting sensitive information and utilizing appropriate authentication mechanisms.

Integrating AI Services into chatbots isn't simply about adding features; it's about building a more intelligent, responsive, and user-friendly conversational experience.

Through careful design, iterative development, and continuous monitoring, we can leverage the power of Azure Cognitive Services to create chatbots that go beyond simple keyword matching and truly understand and engage with users in a meaningful way. The journey involves navigating complexities, but the rewards of a sophisticated chatbot far outweigh the challenges, providing a significant boost to user experience and the overall efficiency of applications. Remember to leverage the free tier of Azure to experiment with these services and gain hands-on experience before scaling your solution to larger, production-level deployments. This iterative approach, combined with a thorough understanding of each service's capabilities and limitations, is key to

creating successful and robust
conversational AI applications.

Designing Effective and Engaging Conversational AI Experiences

Building upon the enhanced capabilities of our chatbot, integrating LUIS and the Speech service, we now turn our attention to the crucial aspect of designing effective and engaging conversational AI experiences. Simply integrating powerful AI services isn't enough; the ultimate goal is to create a chatbot that users find intuitive, helpful, and enjoyable to interact with. This section explores best practices for designing user-friendly and effective conversational AI experiences, focusing on key elements of user engagement and overall experience.

One of the most significant factors in creating a positive user experience is designing a clear and concise conversational flow. Avoid overwhelming users with complex menus or overly lengthy responses. The ideal chatbot conversation should be streamlined, guiding users towards their desired outcome efficiently. Consider employing a conversational design framework, like a state machine or dialogue management system, to ensure a logical and predictable interaction. This framework helps to manage the flow of the conversation, anticipating user inputs and guiding them through different paths depending on their needs.

Think of the conversational flow as a journey. The user embarks on this journey with a specific goal in mind –whether it's finding information, completing a task, or simply having a casual conversation. The design of your conversational AI should seamlessly guide the user along this path, providing clear signposts and avoiding dead ends. This requires careful consideration of potential user inputs and how the bot should respond in various scenarios. For

example, if a user asks a question the bot doesn't understand, the response shouldn't be a blunt "I don't understand."
Instead, a more user-friendly response might be, "I'm still learning! Could you rephrase your question, or try asking it in a different way?" This approach not only avoids frustrating the user but also offers opportunities for learning and improvement for the AI model.

Furthermore, the persona of your chatbot plays a crucial role in shaping the user experience. A well-defined persona provides consistency and personality, making the interaction more engaging and memorable. Consider the tone, style, and language used by your chatbot. Is it formal and professional, or informal and friendly? Does it have a specific name and a defined role? These seemingly minor details can significantly impact user perception and satisfaction. A consistent persona enhances the overall experience by building trust and rapport with the user. For instance, a chatbot designed to assist with technical support might adopt a formal and helpful persona, while a chatbot for customer service might have a more friendly and approachable tone.

The key is to ensure that the persona aligns with the brand and the intended audience.

Another critical element of effective conversational AI design is the use of natural language processing (NLP) techniques to enhance understanding. While keyword-based matching can suffice for simple interactions, leveraging more advanced NLP capabilities significantly improves the bot's ability to interpret user intent and respond appropriately. This includes handling variations in phrasing, slang, and colloquialisms. The more accurately the bot understands the user's input, the more effective and satisfying the interaction becomes. This requires careful training of the NLP model using a large and diverse dataset of user utterances, ensuring that it can handle a wide range of variations in language.

Beyond understanding, the chatbot's response is equally crucial. Responses should be clear, concise, and relevant to the user's input. Avoid using jargon or technical terms that the user might not understand. Instead, opt for plain language that is easy to comprehend. Moreover, the chatbot should be able to provide helpful and accurate information, addressing the user's query effectively. Consider incorporating visual elements like images, buttons, and cards to enhance the user experience and provide additional context. Visuals can break up large blocks of text, making the information easier to digest and more engaging. They can also help to convey information more effectively, especially when dealing with complex topics or instructions.

Error handling and fallback mechanisms are essential components of a robust and user-friendly conversational AI system. The chatbot should gracefully handle situations where it doesn't understand the user's input, providing clear and helpful guidance on how to rephrase or reformulate the question. Instead of simply stating "I don't understand," the chatbot could offer suggestions or guide the user towards alternative pathways. This proactive approach ensures a smooth and frustration-free user experience, even when unexpected inputs arise. Implementing these mechanisms shows users that the system is robust and can handle unexpected situations, building trust and enhancing the overall experience.

Testing and iteration are crucial throughout the design and development process. Regularly testing the chatbot with real users and gathering feedback is vital for identifying areas for improvement.

This feedback can be used to refine the
conversational flow, improve the accuracy of the NLP

model, and enhance the overall user experience. By
iteratively refining the chatbot based on user feedback, you can create a system that is both effective and engaging. Tools such as the Azure Bot Service offer features for analyzing chatbot interactions, providing valuable insights into user behavior and common pain points. This data can then be used to inform design decisions and improve the overall quality of the chatbot.

Personalization is another key factor contributing to a more engaging experience. Where possible and appropriate,
incorporating elements of personalization can significantly improve user satisfaction. This could involve remembering previous interactions, tailoring responses based on user preferences, or using the user's name to create a more
personalized experience. Such

personalization makes the interaction feel more natural and human-like, thereby
enhancing user engagement and building stronger
relationships. However, it's crucial to maintain user privacy and adhere to data protection regulations when implementing personalization features. Transparency about data collection and usage is paramount.

Finally, accessibility should be a paramount consideration in designing conversational AI experiences. Ensuring that the chatbot is accessible to users with disabilities is not only ethically responsible but also expands the potential user base. This involves considering various accessibility needs, including providing alternative text for images, ensuring compatibility with screen readers, and supporting different input methods. Designing for accessibility not only promotes inclusivity but also reinforces the brand's commitment to user-centric design. In the long run, a more inclusive design usually results

in a better user experience for
everyone.

Designing effective and engaging conversational AI
experiences requires a holistic approach, combining
technical expertise with a deep understanding of user needs and expectations. By focusing on clear conversational flow, well-defined persona, advanced NLP capabilities, informative responses, robust error handling, iterative
testing, and accessibility, you can create chatbots that are not only functional but also delightful to interact with.

Remember, the goal is not just to build a chatbot; it is to create a positive and valuable experience for the end user, strengthening their relationship with your brand or service.

Leverage the power of Azure's robust tools and services, coupled with thoughtful design principles, to craft conversational AI that truly engages and delights its users.

By constantly monitoring, iterating, and refining your bot based on user feedback, you can create a truly exceptional user experience that will drive engagement and success.

Fairness Reliability Privacy Inclusiveness Transparency and Accountability

The development and deployment of artificial intelligence (AI) systems carry significant ethical responsibilities.
Microsoft, recognizing this, has established a comprehensive set of Responsible AI principles that guide the creation and use of AI across its products and services. These principles aren't merely aspirational statements; they're actionable guidelines that must be integrated into every stage of the AI lifecycle, from initial conception to ongoing monitoring and maintenance. Understanding and implementing these
principles is crucial for anyone

working with AI, especially those preparing for the AI-900 exam.

At the heart of Microsoft's Responsible AI principles lie six key pillars: Fairness, Reliability, Privacy, Inclusiveness, Transparency, and Accountability. Let's delve into each of these pillars, exploring their significance and how they manifest in practical applications.

Fairness:
Fairness in AI means ensuring that AI systems don't discriminate against any particular group or individual. This is a significant challenge because AI systems learn from data, and if that data reflects existing societal biases, the AI system will likely perpetuate and even amplify those biases.
For example, an AI system trained on hiring data from a company with a history of gender discrimination might inadvertently score female candidates lower than male candidates, even if their qualifications are identical. To mitigate this, developers must carefully curate training datasets to ensure they represent a diverse range

of
populations and actively work to
identify and remove biases from both
data and algorithms. Techniques like
data

augmentation, algorithmic fairness checks, and rigorous testing can help ensure fairness. Furthermore, regular audits of AI systems are crucial to monitor for unintended biases that may emerge over time. The focus should be on creating systems that treat all individuals equitably, regardless of their background or characteristics.

Reliability and Safety:
Reliable and safe AI systems consistently perform as expected and do not pose risks to users or the broader community. Achieving this requires rigorous testing and validation throughout the development process. This includes unit testing, integration testing, and user acceptance testing. Moreover, robust monitoring systems are needed to detect and respond to unexpected behavior or errors in deployed systems. Consider a self-driving car: its AI system must

be incredibly reliable and safe to prevent accidents. This demands extensive testing in various scenarios and the development of fail-safe mechanisms to handle unexpected events. Safety and
reliability must be prioritized from the outset, with
continuous improvement based on feedback and ongoing monitoring.

Privacy:
Protecting user privacy is paramount in the age of AI. AI systems often process vast amounts of personal data, making it crucial to implement robust privacy safeguards.
These safeguards include data anonymization techniques, differential privacy (adding noise to data to obscure
individual identities while preserving statistical properties), and federated learning (training models on decentralized data without directly accessing sensitive information). Compliance with relevant privacy regulations, such as GDPR and CCPA, is essential. For example, an AI system analyzing medical records

must ensure patient
confidentiality by employing strong
encryption and access control
mechanisms. Transparency in how
data is collected,

used, and protected is equally
vital to building trust with users.

Inclusiveness:
Inclusive AI systems are designed and
developed to be accessible and
beneficial to people from all
backgrounds and abilities. This
involves considering diverse
perspectives during the development
process and ensuring the system
works effectively for users with
varying levels of technical proficiency
or disabilities. For instance, an AI-
powered translation tool should be
capable of handling a wide range of
languages and dialects to be truly
inclusive.
Similarly, an AI-driven
accessibility tool should cater to
users with visual, auditory, or
motor impairments.
Accessibility testing and user
feedback are essential to
identify and address any

usability challenges faced by different user groups.

Transparency:
Transparency in AI involves making the decision-making processes of AI systems understandable and explainable. This is crucial for building trust and accountability. Explainable AI (XAI) techniques are designed to shed light on how an AI system arrives at a particular decision. For instance, instead of simply providing a loan application rejection, a transparent system might explain the factors that contributed to the decision, allowing users to understand and address any shortcomings. Documenting the data used, the algorithms employed, and the system's limitations are all key aspects of transparency. Open communication about the capabilities and limitations of AI systems fosters trust and allows for informed decision-making.

Accountability:
Accountability in AI means establishing clear lines of

responsibility for the outcomes of AI systems. This involves identifying who is responsible for the system's design, development, deployment, and ongoing performance.

When problems arise, it's crucial to be able to trace back the source of the issue and determine who is accountable for addressing it. This necessitates establishing clear roles, responsibilities, and processes for handling potential problems or biases identified post-deployment. Regular audits, impact assessments, and the establishment of grievance mechanisms are all key elements of accountability.

Implementing these six principles isn't a one-time task but rather an ongoing process that requires continuous monitoring, evaluation, and adaptation. As AI technology evolves, so too must our understanding and implementation of responsible AI practices. By embracing these principles, we can harness the power of AI while mitigating its potential risks and ensuring a more equitable and beneficial future. The AI-900 exam emphasizes these principles, highlighting their importance in building responsible and ethical AI systems. Thorough understanding of these principles will not only enhance your exam preparation but also equip you with the necessary knowledge and awareness to contribute to the development of trustworthy and beneficial AI solutions. Remember that the ethical considerations surrounding AI are not static; they are continuously evolving as technology advances and societal understanding deepens. Staying informed and engaging in ongoing ethical discussions is essential for responsible AI development.

Mitigating Bias in AI Systems

Building fair and unbiased AI
systems is paramount. The very
data used to train these systems
can reflect existing societal biases,
leading to discriminatory
outcomes.
Therefore, mitigating bias requires a
multi-faceted approach, integrated
throughout the entire AI lifecycle.
This isn't
merely a technical challenge; it's a
societal one, demanding careful
consideration and proactive measures.
The AI-900 exam stresses this,
reflecting the growing awareness of
the ethical implications of biased AI.

One crucial strategy involves careful
data preprocessing. Before any
algorithm sees the data, it's vital to
identify and address potential biases
embedded within. This might

involve scrutinizing the data collection process itself. Was the data gathered in a way that systematically excluded certain groups? For example, a facial recognition system trained primarily on images of light-skinned individuals will likely perform poorly on darker-skinned individuals, reflecting a bias in the dataset. Similarly, datasets for loan applications that predominantly include data from higher-income groups will likely perpetuate existing inequalities in lending practices. Identifying and addressing such sampling biases is crucial.

Data augmentation techniques can also help mitigate bias. If a dataset underrepresents a specific demographic group, strategically adding more data points representing that group can help balance the representation. However, it's crucial to ensure the augmented data is representative and doesn't introduce new biases. Simply duplicating existing data points from the underrepresented group wouldn't address the underlying issue; it would only artificially inflate its representation. Effective data augmentation requires careful consideration and often involves specialized techniques to generate synthetic data that accurately reflects the

characteristics of the underrepresented group. This is a complex process requiring domain expertise and rigorous validation.

Another key aspect of data preprocessing involves addressing noisy or irrelevant features. Data might contain attributes that, while seemingly innocuous, can indirectly contribute to bias. For instance, an AI system predicting job applicant suitability might inadvertently rely on features such as zip code, which can be correlated with socioeconomic factors and lead to discriminatory outcomes. Identifying and removing or transforming such features is crucial.

This might involve sophisticated feature engineering techniques or dimensionality reduction methods to remove or combine features that contribute to bias.

The choice of algorithm itself can significantly impact bias. Some algorithms are inherently more susceptible to bias than others. For example, linear regression models, while simple and interpretable, can be sensitive to outliers and correlated features, potentially amplifying existing biases in the data. More sophisticated algorithms, such as tree-based models or neural networks, might be more robust to noise and outliers but can still be susceptible to bias if the data itself is biased. Therefore, careful algorithm selection, considering the specific characteristics of the data and the desired outcomes, is crucial. Moreover, careful tuning of hyperparameters for the chosen algorithm plays a vital role in minimizing bias.

Beyond data preprocessing and algorithm selection, post-processing techniques can also mitigate bias. These methods focus on adjusting the output of the AI system to address any remaining bias detected after training. One such technique is recalibration, where the model's predictions are adjusted to ensure fairness across different demographic groups. For instance, if a loan application prediction model consistently underestimates the creditworthiness of applicants from certain backgrounds, recalibration techniques can adjust the model's output to compensate for this bias. However, it's important to understand that post-processing methods can only compensate for bias; they don't address the root cause.

Therefore, they should be used in conjunction with data preprocessing and careful algorithm selection, forming a comprehensive strategy.

Another post-processing technique is adversarial debiasing. This method involves training a separate model, the "adversarial model," to identify and counteract the biases in the main model's predictions. The adversarial model acts as a critic, trying to detect and correct any unfairness in the main model's output. This approach can be particularly effective in complex scenarios where biases are subtle and difficult to detect directly. The effectiveness of adversarial debiasing depends heavily on the design of both the main and adversarial models and requires careful tuning and evaluation.

Monitoring and evaluation are essential ongoing processes in mitigating bias. Even after deploying an AI system, it's crucial to continuously monitor its performance across different demographic groups and identify any emerging biases. This requires establishing clear metrics to measure fairness and setting up systems for ongoing monitoring and evaluation. For example, analyzing the model's predictions on a representative test set can reveal biases not apparent during training.

Regular audits and impact assessments are crucial to ensure the system remains fair and unbiased over time. This iterative process of monitoring, evaluation, and adjustment is vital for ensuring the long-term fairness of AI

systems. The AI-900 exam
highlights the importance of
continuous monitoring and
evaluation as integral
components of responsible AI
development.

Transparency and explainability are
crucial in building trust and
understanding in AI systems.
Knowing how an AI
system makes its decisions is essential
for identifying and mitigating bias.
Therefore, choosing models that are
inherently interpretable or developing
techniques to explain complex
models' decisions are vital steps.
Techniques like LIME (Local
Interpretable Model-agnostic
Explanations) or SHAP (SHapley
Additive exPlanations) can help
provide insights into the factors
contributing to a model's predictions,
highlighting potential biases. This
transparency allows for better scrutiny
and facilitates the identification and

correction of any bias. Moreover, transparent models foster accountability, enabling us to trace the origin of any bias to specific factors in the data or algorithm design. This transparency is crucial for building trust and ensuring ethical development and use of AI systems.

Beyond the technical strategies, fostering a culture of ethical AI development is crucial. This requires training data scientists, engineers, and other stakeholders on the importance of fairness and bias mitigation. It also involves establishing clear guidelines and policies regarding responsible AI within organizations. Microsoft's Responsible AI principles provide a valuable framework for this. Regular workshops, training sessions, and ethical review boards can help ensure that ethical considerations are embedded into the design, development, and deployment of AI systems. A culture of continuous learning and improvement is crucial to ensure that AI systems are developed and used responsibly, minimizing the risks of bias and promoting fairness. The AI-900 exam emphasizes the importance of understanding and implementing these principles, encouraging a proactive approach to ethical AI development.

In conclusion, mitigating bias in AI systems requires a holistic approach that encompasses data preprocessing, algorithm selection, post-processing techniques, and continuous monitoring and evaluation. It also necessitates fostering a culture of ethical AI development within organizations and across the wider AI community. By carefully considering these aspects, we can build AI systems that are not only technically robust but also fair, equitable, and beneficial to society as a whole. Understanding and implementing these strategies is not merely important for passing the AI-900 exam; it's crucial for ensuring a responsible and ethical future for AI. The constant evolution of AI technology necessitates a continuous effort to refine our understanding and implementation of these techniques, promoting fairness and responsible innovation.

Ensuring Reliability and Safety in AI Systems

Ensuring the reliability and safety of AI systems is paramount, especially as these systems become increasingly integrated into critical infrastructure and decision-making processes. This requires a robust and multifaceted approach that goes beyond simply achieving high accuracy on training data. We need to consider the potential for unexpected failures, vulnerabilities, and unintended consequences, and design systems that are resilient, safe, and trustworthy. This involves a rigorous process of testing, validation, and ongoing monitoring.

One crucial aspect of ensuring reliability is thorough testing.
This goes beyond simply evaluating performance metrics like accuracy or

precision. We must perform a variety of tests to assess different aspects of the system's behavior. Unit testing focuses on individual components of the AI system, verifying that each part functions correctly in isolation. Integration testing examines how these components interact, ensuring seamless communication and data flow. System testing evaluates the entire system as a whole, considering its interactions with other systems and its overall performance under different conditions.

Beyond functional testing, we also need to consider robustness testing. This involves subjecting the AI system to a range of inputs, including unusual, unexpected, and even adversarial examples. The goal is to identify vulnerabilities and weaknesses, understanding how the system behaves under stress. Stress testing simulates heavy loads and extreme conditions to determine the system's resilience and stability. This can involve increasing the volume of data processed, introducing noisy data, or manipulating input parameters. The results of these tests are critical in identifying potential points of failure and areas requiring improvement.

A particularly important area of robustness testing is adversarial machine learning. This focuses on the potential for malicious actors to manipulate the inputs to the AI system to cause it to produce incorrect or harmful outputs. For example, a self-driving car's image recognition system could be tricked by subtly altering the image of a stop sign, leading to a dangerous situation. Developing techniques to detect and mitigate these attacks is crucial for the safety and reliability of AI systems, especially those deployed in security-sensitive applications. This requires a deep understanding of the AI model's inner workings and its vulnerabilities to manipulation. Methods such as adversarial training – training the model on adversarial examples to make it more resilient – are being actively researched and developed.

Validation is a crucial step to ensure that the AI system meets its specified requirements and performs as intended in its intended environment. This involves a comprehensive evaluation process, typically involving a diverse team of experts. The validation process should include a review of the system's design, development, and testing procedures. Independent verification is essential, involving experts who were not directly involved in the development process to offer an unbiased assessment. Formal verification techniques, often employing mathematical models, can be used to formally prove certain properties of the system, such as its correctness or safety.

Once the AI system is deployed, ongoing monitoring is essential to maintain its reliability and safety. This involves continuously tracking the system's performance and identifying potential issues. Monitoring should cover various aspects, including performance metrics, error rates, resource utilization, and user feedback. Real-time monitoring allows for the immediate detection and response to anomalies or failures. The data collected from monitoring can be used to identify patterns, predict potential problems, and refine the system's performance over time. This iterative process is crucial in adapting to evolving conditions and ensuring the long-term reliability of the system. Effective monitoring necessitates robust logging and alerting mechanisms, promptly notifying relevant personnel of critical events or deviations from expected behavior. The implementation of these systems should be a top priority in any responsible AI development.

Furthermore, explainability and interpretability play a crucial role in ensuring reliability and safety. It is often difficult to understand how complex AI systems arrive at their decisions, which can make it challenging to identify errors or biases. However, understanding the reasoning behind a system's output is critical for building trust and ensuring accountability. Techniques such as LIME (Local Interpretable Model-agnostic Explanations) and SHAP (SHapley Additive exPlanations) are being developed to help explain the predictions of complex AI models. These methods aim to provide insights into the factors that contribute to a particular prediction, allowing developers to identify potential problems or biases. The goal is not necessarily to fully understand every aspect of a complex model, but to provide enough insight to diagnose issues and build confidence in the system's reliability. Increased transparency helps to improve both

the debugging and the trustworthiness
of the deployed model.

The development of robust safety
mechanisms is critical, especially
for high-stakes applications. This
might involve

incorporating redundancy or fail-safes into the system's design. For example, a self-driving car might have multiple sensors and processing units, with backup systems in case of failures. Similarly, critical decisions made by AI systems should be reviewed by human operators, ensuring that a human-in-the-loop mechanism is in place to prevent catastrophic errors. The human oversight element is particularly important for applications with significant societal impact, allowing for intervention when necessary and maintaining a level of control over potentially autonomous systems. Defining clear protocols for human intervention in case of system malfunctions is vital.

Data governance and security are also crucial factors in ensuring the reliability and safety of AI systems. Data used to train and operate AI systems must be carefully managed and protected to prevent unauthorized access, modification, or deletion. Robust security measures are necessary to protect against cyberattacks and data breaches, ensuring the integrity and confidentiality of sensitive information.

Furthermore, the data itself should be high-quality, free from errors and inconsistencies, and representative of the intended application domain. Addressing issues of bias, incompleteness, and inconsistency in the data set itself is critical for minimizing error propagation and ensuring the reliability of the AI model's output.

The ethical considerations surrounding AI safety and reliability must also be carefully considered. Transparency and accountability are vital in building trust. Users should have a clear understanding of how the system works and how decisions are made. Clear lines of accountability should be established, defining who is responsible for the system's actions and outcomes. This also extends to the responsibility of continuously monitoring and improving the system to address evolving ethical challenges. The ethical framework

should be clearly documented
and readily available for review,
ensuring transparency and
facilitating external audits.

Finally, continuous improvement is
key to maintaining the reliability and
safety of AI systems. Regular updates,
patches, and retraining are necessary
to address
vulnerabilities, improve performance,
and adapt to changing conditions. A
well-defined process for managing
updates and ensuring system stability
is essential. This iterative process
ensures that the AI system remains
robust, secure, and aligned with
evolving ethical standards and user
requirements. This cyclical approach
ensures continuous refinement and
adaptation, crucial for maintaining the
long-term reliability and safety of the
AI system in a dynamically changing
environment. A strong commitment to
continuous improvement

demonstrates a responsible approach to AI development.

Protecting Privacy in AI Systems

Building upon the critical aspects of reliability and safety discussed previously, we now turn our attention to another cornerstone of responsible AI: privacy. As AI systems increasingly process and analyze personal data, safeguarding user privacy becomes not just an ethical imperative, but a legal and business necessity. The potential for misuse of sensitive information is significant, and robust privacy-preserving techniques are crucial to maintaining public trust and avoiding legal repercussions. This section explores various methods for protecting user privacy within the context of AI systems, focusing on techniques that balance the need for data-driven insights with the fundamental right to privacy.

One fundamental approach to protecting privacy is **data anonymization**. This involves removing or altering personally identifiable information (PII) from datasets used to train and operate AI models. However, the effectiveness of anonymization is dependent on the techniques employed and the sophistication of potential adversaries. Simple techniques like removing names and addresses may not be sufficient, as sophisticated attackers might be able to re-identify individuals through the combination of seemingly innocuous attributes such as age, gender, location, and purchasing habits. Therefore, more advanced anonymization techniques, such as k-anonymity and l-diversity, are often employed. K-anonymity ensures that each record in a dataset is indistinguishable from at least k-1 other records based on a set of quasi-identifiers. L-diversity adds an additional layer of protection by requiring that within each group of k-anonymous records, there is sufficient diversity in sensitive attributes. For example, in a healthcare dataset, l-diversity

might ensure that within each k-anonymous group, there is a diverse range of diagnoses, preventing an attacker from easily inferring sensitive health information about an individual.

Despite their strengths, even these advanced anonymization techniques are not foolproof. The potential for re-identification remains, particularly with the increasing availability of large public datasets and sophisticated data linkage techniques. Moreover, the process of anonymization itself can introduce biases and inaccuracies into the data, potentially affecting the performance and fairness of the AI system. It's crucial to carefully evaluate the trade-offs between the level of privacy protection achieved and the potential impact on data utility. A well-defined anonymization strategy must be carefully tailored to the specific context of the AI application, considering the sensitivity of the data, the potential risks of re-identification, and the acceptable level of data utility. Regular audits and evaluations are essential to ensure the ongoing effectiveness of the anonymization process.

Another powerful technique for protecting privacy is **differential privacy**. Unlike anonymization, which aims to remove PII entirely, differential privacy adds carefully calibrated noise to the output of a query on a dataset. This noise is designed to make it extremely difficult to infer information about any individual record within the dataset, while still preserving the overall statistical properties of the data. The amount of noise added is carefully controlled by a parameter known as "epsilon," which determines the trade-off between privacy and accuracy. A smaller epsilon value provides stronger privacy guarantees but may lead to less accurate results. Conversely, a larger epsilon value allows for more accurate results but sacrifices some privacy. Differential privacy is particularly effective in scenarios where queries are made against sensitive datasets, such as those containing medical or financial information.

The strength of differential privacy lies in its rigorous mathematical foundation, providing provable privacy guarantees even against powerful adversaries with access to auxiliary information. This makes it a highly robust technique for protecting sensitive data while still enabling useful data analysis. However, the application of differential privacy can be challenging, requiring careful design and implementation to minimize the impact on data utility. Moreover, choosing the appropriate epsilon value often involves a delicate balance between privacy and accuracy, requiring careful consideration of the specific application and risk tolerance. The practical implementation of differential privacy often involves specialized algorithms and techniques that must be carefully chosen to suit the specific data and query characteristics.

Federated learning
offers a fundamentally different approach to privacy preservation. Instead of centralizing data in a single location, federated learning allows AI models to be trained collaboratively across multiple decentralized devices or servers, without directly sharing the underlying data. Each device or server trains a local model on its own data, and only the model parameters (weights and biases) are shared with a central server for aggregation. The central server then aggregates these local model parameters to create a global model, which is then distributed back to the participating devices. This process iterates multiple times, allowing the global model to improve over time without ever directly accessing the individual data points.

Federated learning offers several advantages in terms of privacy. Because the raw data never leaves the individual devices, it significantly reduces the risk of data breaches and unauthorized access. This is particularly important in applications involving sensitive data, such as healthcare or finance, where data privacy is paramount. Furthermore, federated learning can enable the training of AI models on significantly larger and more diverse datasets than would be possible with traditional centralized approaches, potentially leading to improved model accuracy and generalization. However, federated learning also presents its own set of challenges. The communication overhead of transferring model parameters between devices can be significant, particularly in low-bandwidth environments. Furthermore, ensuring the convergence and robustness of the global model can be challenging, requiring careful design and optimization of the aggregation process.

The choice of privacy-preserving technique depends heavily on the specific context of the AI application. For instance, data anonymization might be suitable for datasets where re-identification risk is relatively low, and the impact of data utility loss is acceptable. Conversely, differential privacy may be preferred for highly sensitive data where strong privacy guarantees are essential, even at the cost of some accuracy. Federated learning provides an alternative approach that avoids data centralization altogether, but it might not be suitable for applications requiring real-time processing or extremely high accuracy. In many cases, a hybrid approach combining multiple techniques might be the most effective way to achieve a robust balance between privacy and utility.

Finally, it is crucial to remember that the implementation of privacy-preserving techniques is only one aspect of a
broader approach to responsible AI. Transparency,
accountability, and user consent are

equally important. Users should be
clearly informed about how their data
is being collected, used, and
protected. Mechanisms for auditing
and

verifying the effectiveness of privacy-preserving techniques are also necessary to build and maintain trust. Ongoing research and development in privacy-enhancing technologies are continuously evolving, and it is essential for AI practitioners to stay abreast of the latest advancements and best practices to ensure the responsible development and deployment of AI systems that protect user privacy. The future of AI hinges on the successful integration of ethical considerations, including robust privacy protection, into the design and deployment of these powerful technologies. The responsible use of AI requires a multifaceted approach, embracing ethical principles throughout the entire lifecycle of development and deployment. By adopting these practices, we can harness the transformative potential of AI while safeguarding individual rights and

building a more trustworthy and
equitable future.

Promoting Inclusiveness and Transparency in AI

Building on the vital principles of privacy and reliability, we now delve into the crucial aspects of inclusiveness and transparency in the development and deployment of AI systems. These two principles are intrinsically linked, forming the bedrock of responsible AI and ensuring equitable access and understanding of AI's impact. Without inclusiveness, AI systems risk perpetuating and amplifying existing societal biases, leading to unfair or discriminatory outcomes. A lack of transparency, on the other hand, undermines trust and accountability, hindering the ability to identify and rectify errors or biases within the system.

Together, inclusiveness and transparency ensure that AI benefits all members of society and operates in a fair and accountable manner.

The quest for inclusiveness in AI begins with the data itself.
AI systems are trained on data, and if that data reflects existing societal biases—whether conscious or unconscious—the resulting system will inevitably inherit and potentially exacerbate those biases. For example, facial recognition systems trained primarily on images of light-skinned individuals have demonstrably lower accuracy rates when identifying individuals with darker skin tones. This is not simply a technical shortcoming; it's a consequence of biased datasets that fail to represent the diversity of the human population. To mitigate this, we must strive for data diversity. This involves actively seeking out and incorporating data from a wide range of sources and

demographics, ensuring that the data accurately reflects the population the system is intended to serve. This is not merely a matter of achieving numerical parity; it requires careful consideration of the nuances within diverse populations, ensuring that subgroups are not inadvertently marginalized or misrepresented.

Furthermore, data collection methods themselves must be carefully scrutinized. Are the methods employed likely to underrepresent certain groups? Are there systematic biases in how data is collected, labeled, and curated? Addressing these questions requires a thorough understanding of potential biases at each stage of the data pipeline, from data
acquisition to data cleaning and preprocessing. This requires a multidisciplinary approach, involving not only data
scientists and engineers, but also social scientists, ethicists, and community members who can provide valuable insights into the potential impact of data collection methods on different groups. The development of robust data governance frameworks is

crucial to ensuring data quality, diversity, and ethical compliance. Such frameworks should define clear procedures for data collection, storage, processing, and disposal, along with mechanisms for identifying and mitigating potential biases.

Beyond data diversity, inclusiveness in AI extends to the development and deployment processes themselves. Diverse teams of engineers, designers, and researchers bring a broader range of perspectives and experiences, making it more likely that potential biases will be identified and addressed during the development process. Involving individuals from underrepresented groups throughout the AI lifecycle helps ensure that the resulting systems are both effective and equitable. This encompasses participation in design, testing, evaluation, and ongoing monitoring of the system's performance and impact on different populations.

This inclusive approach fosters a sense of ownership and accountability, further improving the likelihood of creating AI systems that are both beneficial and fair to all.

Transparency in AI is equally crucial for building trust and accountability. AI systems, particularly complex machine learning models, can often be opaque, making it difficult to understand how they arrive at their decisions. This "black box" nature makes it challenging to identify and correct errors or biases, and it can erode public trust in the technology. This is where Explainable AI (XAI) comes into play. XAI aims to develop techniques that make the decision-making processes of AI systems more understandable and interpretable. Different approaches exist, ranging from simpler models that are inherently more transparent to more sophisticated techniques that provide explanations for the predictions made by complex models.

These explanations could take the form of visualizations, rule-based explanations, or natural language summaries, tailoring the explanations to the specific audience and context.

The choice of XAI technique depends on the specific AI system and its intended application. For high-stakes decisions, such as loan applications or medical diagnoses, a high degree of transparency is critical, demanding more rigorous methods for explanation. In other cases, simpler explanations might suffice. However, it is crucial to remember that XAI is not simply a technical problem; it requires careful consideration of ethical and societal implications. Explanations need to be accurate, complete, and easily understandable to the intended audience.

Furthermore, there is a need for standardized methods for evaluating the quality and trustworthiness of XAI explanations. Ongoing research in this area is essential to developing robust and effective techniques

that promote transparency and
build trust in AI systems.

Transparency extends beyond XAI to
the entire lifecycle of AI development
and deployment. Users should have a
clear

understanding of how an AI system works, what data it uses, and what its limitations are. This requires clear and accessible documentation, along with mechanisms for users to provide feedback and raise concerns. Transparency also involves responsible data governance, ensuring that data is used ethically and responsibly. This includes establishing clear guidelines on data collection, usage, and storage, and implementing robust security measures to protect data from unauthorized access or misuse. Transparency also involves proactive communication about the capabilities and

limitations of AI systems, avoiding over-hyping their

capabilities and managing user expectations. By being

upfront about potential biases and limitations, we can foster a more realistic understanding of AI's potential and mitigate the risk of misplaced trust or unrealistic expectations.

Accountability is closely intertwined with transparency and inclusiveness. It is crucial to establish clear lines of responsibility for the decisions made by AI systems. Who is accountable when an AI system makes a mistake or exhibits bias? This requires a multi-faceted approach, involving clear guidelines, robust auditing mechanisms, and effective oversight processes. It necessitates assigning responsibility to developers, deployers, and users, clearly defining roles and responsibilities throughout the AI system lifecycle. This includes establishing clear mechanisms for reporting issues, investigating complaints, and implementing corrective actions. Accountability is not simply a legal requirement; it is essential for building public trust and fostering the responsible development and deployment of AI. By addressing accountability transparently and comprehensively, we can ensure that

AI technologies serve the greater good.

In conclusion, promoting inclusiveness and transparency in AI is a continuous process requiring a commitment to ethical principles at every stage of development and deployment. This involves actively seeking diverse datasets, employing XAI techniques to enhance understanding, establishing robust data governance frameworks, and building diverse and inclusive teams. By prioritizing these principles, we can harness the transformative power of AI while mitigating the risks of bias and ensuring that AI benefits all members of society. The path towards truly responsible AI requires not just technical expertise but also a deep understanding of ethical considerations, social impact, and the importance of fostering trust and accountability. The future of AI depends on our collective commitment to these essential principles. Only through diligent effort and a commitment to ongoing learning and adaptation can we build an AI future that is both innovative and ethically sound. The journey towards responsible AI is not a destination, but rather an ongoing commitment to continuous improvement and a steadfast dedication to ethical practice.

Introduction to Azure Machine Learning Studio

Azure Machine Learning Studio (MLS) represents a significant advancement in making the power of machine learning accessible to a broader audience, even those without extensive programming experience. It provides a visual, drag-and-drop interface, significantly lowering the barrier to entry for building and deploying machine learning models.

This contrasts sharply with traditional machine learning development, which often necessitates proficiency in programming languages like Python or R. MLS empowers users to design, train, and evaluate models using a user-friendly graphical environment, making complex tasks more manageable and intuitive.

The core strength of MLS lies in its ability to abstract away the intricacies of coding. Instead of writing complex lines of code, users can visually construct their machine learning pipelines by selecting and connecting modules. These modules represent various stages in the machine learning process, from data ingestion and preprocessing to model training, evaluation, and deployment. This visual approach not only simplifies the development process but also allows for better understanding and transparency of the model's construction. Users can easily track the flow of data and transformations, facilitating debugging and model refinement.

Within MLS, users can access a vast library of pre-built modules. These modules offer pre-configured algorithms for various machine learning tasks, including regression, classification, clustering, and anomaly detection. This pre-built functionality is particularly valuable for users new to machine learning, as it eliminates the need to implement

algorithms from scratch. Furthermore, it allows them to quickly experiment with different algorithms and compare their performance without needing deep coding expertise. The availability of such pre-built components is key to the Studio's low-code, even no-code, approach to ML model development.

One of the critical aspects of MLS is its seamless integration with other Azure services. For instance, users can easily connect to Azure Blob Storage for data ingestion, leveraging the scalability and reliability of Azure's cloud infrastructure. Similarly, deploying trained models can be accomplished via integration with Azure App Service or Azure Kubernetes Service (AKS), providing robust and scalable deployment options for various application needs. This tight integration within the Azure ecosystem makes it convenient for users already working within the Microsoft cloud environment.

The process of building a model in MLS typically begins with data import. Users can connect to various data sources, including local files, Azure Blob Storage, and SQL databases. Once the data is imported, it can be preprocessed using a range of built-in modules. These modules allow for tasks like data cleaning, transformation, and feature engineering. Data cleaning involves handling missing values, outliers, and inconsistencies. Transformation includes tasks such as scaling, normalization, and encoding categorical variables. Feature engineering involves creating new features from existing ones to improve model accuracy. These preprocessing steps are crucial for ensuring the quality and effectiveness of the model. MLS simplifies these often complex tasks by providing intuitive graphical tools.

After data preprocessing, the user selects a machine learning algorithm appropriate for the task. MLS offers a wide range of algorithms, categorized by task type (classification, regression, clustering, etc.). The choice of algorithm depends on the nature of the problem and the type of data being used.

For example, for a classification task, a user might choose from algorithms such as logistic regression, support vector machines, or decision trees. For regression, options could include linear regression, polynomial regression, or support vector regression. MLS provides clear documentation and descriptions for each algorithm, making it easier for users to make informed decisions.

Once the algorithm is selected, the user can configure its parameters. Many parameters govern the behavior of the algorithm, and understanding them is crucial for achieving optimal results. MLS provides intuitive interfaces for setting these parameters, often with default values suitable for beginners. However, more experienced users can adjust these parameters to fine-tune the model's performance. This allows users to balance simplicity with fine-grained control over their model building process.

Model training is performed within MLS by executing the pipeline. This involves sending the processed data to the selected algorithm, which then learns the patterns in the data.
The training process can take some time, depending on the size of the data and the complexity of the algorithm. MLS provides progress indicators to keep the user informed about the training status. The completed training process generates a trained model that can then be evaluated and deployed.

Model evaluation is a critical step in the machine learning process. It involves assessing the performance of the trained model using appropriate metrics. These metrics depend on the type of problem being addressed. For classification, common metrics include accuracy, precision, recall, and F1-score. For regression, metrics such as mean squared error (MSE)

and R-squared are often used. MLS
provides tools for

evaluating models automatically, displaying the results in a clear and concise manner. This allows users to compare the performance of different models and select the best one.

Once a satisfactory model is obtained, it can be deployed using MLS. Deployment involves making the model available for use in an application. MLS offers various deployment options, allowing users to deploy their models to different environments depending on their needs. These options include deploying the model as a web service, a batch processing job, or integration with other Azure services. The deployment process is simplified by the user-friendly interface of MLS, making it accessible even to less experienced users.

Beyond the core functionalities described above, MLS offers features that enhance collaboration and reproducibility.
Users can save their experiments, share them with
colleagues, and reproduce results at any time. This feature is valuable for documenting the model development process and ensuring that the results are consistent and reliable.
Furthermore, MLS's integration with Azure DevOps makes it possible to manage the entire model lifecycle, from
development to deployment and monitoring, using industry-standard tools.

One of the most significant advantages of MLS is its support for experimentation. Users can easily try different
algorithms, preprocessing techniques, and parameter
settings, comparing their results to find the optimal model for a specific task. This iterative process of experimentation is essential for achieving high performance in

machine learning. MLS makes this process streamlined and efficient. The visual nature of the platform helps users understand the impact of different choices on model performance, allowing for informed decision-making.

Finally, MLS provides robust monitoring capabilities. After deploying a model, it's crucial to track its performance in a real-world setting. MLS integrates with Azure Monitor, allowing users to monitor key metrics, such as latency and throughput, ensuring the model is performing as expected.
Early detection of performance issues can prevent
disruptions and ensure the ongoing reliability of the
deployed models. This monitoring capability is vital for the long-term success of any machine learning project.

In summary, Azure Machine Learning Studio empowers both novice and experienced users to navigate the world of machine learning. Its visual, drag-and-drop interface,
extensive library of pre-built modules, and tight integration with other Azure

services make it a powerful and versatile tool for developing and deploying machine learning models. Its focus on ease of use and accessibility positions it as a key component in democratizing machine learning and making its capabilities available to a wider audience. Its role in the Azure ecosystem ensures that users can leverage the full power of the cloud for their machine learning initiatives.

Streamlining the Machine Learning Workflow

Building upon the accessibility and ease of use introduced by Azure Machine Learning Studio, Azure Automated Machine Learning (AutoML) represents a further leap forward in democratizing machine learning. AutoML significantly streamlines the often complex and iterative process of building, training, and deploying machine learning models. It automates many of the traditionally manual and time-consuming tasks, allowing data scientists and even citizen data scientists to focus on the higher-level aspects of model building, such as feature engineering, model selection, and performance evaluation.

The core benefit of AutoML lies in its ability to automate the selection and tuning of machine learning algorithms.
Traditional machine learning often requires significant experimentation with different algorithms, hyperparameters, and feature engineering techniques to find the optimal model. This process can be both time-consuming and computationally expensive. AutoML, however, leverages advanced algorithms and optimization techniques to automatically explore a vast space of possible model configurations and select the one that best suits the data and the desired objective. This automation significantly reduces the time and effort required to build high-performing models.

Furthermore, AutoML simplifies the process of feature engineering, a crucial step in machine learning that often involves significant domain

expertise. AutoML
automatically identifies relevant
features, transforms them to improve
model performance, and even
generates new
features based on existing ones. This
automation removes a

significant barrier to entry for individuals lacking extensive data science experience.

One of the key strengths of Azure AutoML is its seamless integration with the broader Azure ecosystem. This integration allows users to leverage the power of Azure's cloud infrastructure for model training and deployment. The scalability of the Azure cloud allows AutoML to handle large datasets and complex models that might be challenging to manage on local machines. This scalability is particularly crucial for organizations dealing with big data applications, enabling them to train and deploy models quickly and efficiently.

Let's illustrate the power of AutoML with a concrete example. Imagine a retail company that wants to predict customer churn.

They have a large dataset containing customer demographics, purchase history, and interaction with customer service. Using traditional methods, a data scientist would need to spend considerable time cleaning the data, selecting appropriate features, experimenting with various algorithms (logistic regression, support vector machines, random forests, etc.), tuning hyperparameters for each algorithm, and evaluating the performance of each model. This process is iterative and requires extensive knowledge of machine learning techniques and substantial computational resources.

With AutoML, the process is considerably simplified. The data scientist uploads the dataset to Azure Machine Learning, specifies the target variable (customer churn), and selects the desired performance metric (e.g., accuracy, precision, recall). AutoML then automatically handles the rest: data preprocessing, feature engineering, algorithm selection, hyperparameter tuning, and model training. The system automatically trains multiple models using various algorithms, evaluating their performance based on the specified metric. The results are presented to the data scientist in a user-friendly dashboard, showing the performance of each model, along with key metrics and visualizations. The data scientist can then select the best-performing model and deploy it for prediction. This dramatically reduces the time and expertise required to build a predictive model for customer churn.

The ease of use extends beyond model building. AutoML also simplifies model deployment. Once a model is trained, it can be easily deployed as a web service or integrated into other applications using various deployment options offered by Azure. This simplifies the process of integrating machine learning models into business workflows and making them accessible to other parts of the organization. This integration capability is a vital aspect of making machine learning solutions practical and impactful for business decision-making.

Furthermore, AutoML caters to different skill levels.
Experienced data scientists can use AutoML to accelerate their workflows, freeing them from repetitive tasks and allowing them to focus on more strategic aspects of the project. On the other hand, citizen data scientists or business analysts with limited machine learning expertise can use AutoML to build and deploy models with minimal coding or specialized knowledge. This empowers a wider range of individuals to leverage the power of machine learning within their organizations, fostering a more data-driven culture.

Consider another scenario: a healthcare provider aiming to predict patient readmission rates. They possess a vast amount of patient data including medical history, diagnoses, treatment details, and demographics. Using AutoML, they can easily upload this data, specify readmission as the target variable, and let the system automatically handle the complexities of model building. The system will explore various algorithms, tune parameters, and present the results with detailed performance metrics. This allows the healthcare provider to identify high-risk patients and proactively implement interventions to reduce readmission rates – a significant improvement in patient care and resource allocation. The efficiency gained through AutoML enables the healthcare provider to focus on patient care and strategic decision-making rather than getting bogged down in the complexities of machine learning algorithms.

The versatility of AutoML extends beyond classification and regression tasks. It supports various machine learning tasks including image classification, object detection, natural language processing (NLP), and time series forecasting. This makes it a truly versatile tool applicable across a wide range of industries and applications. For example, in an image classification task, AutoML can automatically train models to identify objects in images, while in an NLP task, it can be used to build models for sentiment analysis, text summarization, or named entity recognition. These capabilities greatly expand the scope and applicability of AutoML within organizations.

Moreover, Azure AutoML offers advanced features that empower users to further customize and control the modeling process. While it automates many tasks, it does not eliminate the role of the data scientist. Experienced users can leverage advanced options to fine-tune the model training process, specifying constraints, algorithm choices, or feature engineering techniques. This gives them the flexibility to tailor the automated process to their specific needs and

domain expertise. This combination of automation and
control is a crucial strength of AutoML, catering to both novice and expert users.

AutoML also facilitates
experimentation and comparison of
different models. It provides tools to
visualize the
performance of various models,
compare their metrics, and analyze
their strengths and weaknesses. This
allows data scientists to make
informed decisions about model
selection, understanding the trade-offs
between different models and
choosing the one that best meets their
specific requirements.
This enhanced transparency and
insight are crucial for building
trust and understanding in the
models generated.

Furthermore, Azure AutoML
promotes responsible AI
practices by providing tools and
features to monitor and evaluate the
fairness, reliability, and explainability
of the models it creates. This focus on
responsible AI is crucial for ensuring

that machine learning models are used ethically and responsibly. The built-in features allow for detecting and mitigating potential bias in the data and models, promoting fairness and transparency in the decision-making process.

In conclusion, Azure Automated Machine Learning is a powerful and versatile tool that significantly simplifies the machine learning workflow. Its automation capabilities reduce the time and expertise required to build, train, and deploy high-performing models, making machine learning accessible to a much broader audience. The seamless integration with the Azure ecosystem, support for various machine learning tasks, and advanced features for customization and responsible AI make it a crucial tool for both novice and expert data scientists, empowering organizations to leverage the full potential of machine learning across various applications. Its role in democratizing access to machine learning and its focus on responsible AI positions AutoML as a significant advancement in the field, driving innovation and efficiency in diverse sectors.

Building Machine Learning Models with Azure Machine Learning Studio

Azure Machine Learning Studio provides a visually intuitive drag-and-drop interface, significantly lowering the barrier to entry for building and deploying machine learning models. This contrasts sharply with the more code-intensive approaches often associated with traditional machine learning development. The platform's graphical nature allows users to focus on the model's logic and data flow rather than getting bogged down in intricate coding details.

This ease of use extends to various stages of the machine learning lifecycle, from data preparation and feature engineering to model training, evaluation, and deployment.

Let's walk through a practical example to illustrate the process. Imagine we're tasked with building a model to predict customer churn for a telecommunications company. We have a dataset containing customer demographics, usage patterns, and churn status. First, we import this dataset into Azure Machine Learning Studio. This can be done by uploading a file directly from our local machine or connecting to various data sources such as Azure Blob Storage, Azure SQL Database, or even pulling data directly from Excel spreadsheets. The flexibility in data ingestion is a key strength of the platform.

Once the data is imported, we can begin the process of data exploration and preprocessing. Azure Machine Learning Studio offers a rich set of modules to handle this. We can use modules to visualize the data distributions, identify missing values, and handle outliers. For instance, we might use the "Data Cleaning" module to handle missing values by imputation, perhaps using the mean or median of the respective feature. Outliers can be addressed through various techniques, including winsorization or trimming, available through other pre-processing modules. Feature scaling and normalization are crucial steps to ensure that features contribute equally to the model's learning process. We might utilize the "Normalize Data" module to scale numerical features to a similar range, preventing features with larger values from dominating the model.

Feature engineering, a crucial aspect of model building, involves creating new features from existing ones to improve model performance. In our churn prediction example, we might create new features such as "average monthly usage" or "percentage of calls dropped" from the existing call detail records. This process might involve using the "Execute R Script" or "Execute Python Script" modules within the

Studio, allowing for greater flexibility in complex feature engineering tasks that may require custom code. This blend of visual workflows and code integration is a hallmark of Azure Machine Learning Studio's flexibility.

Next, we select an appropriate machine learning algorithm.
The choice of algorithm depends on the nature of our
prediction task (in this case, binary classification – churn or no churn). Azure Machine Learning Studio offers a wide range of algorithms, including logistic regression, support vector machines (SVMs), decision trees, random forests, and neural networks. Each algorithm is accessible through a simple drag-and-drop module. We can experiment with different algorithms to find the one that yields the best
performance on our dataset. This involves training the model using a portion of our data (the training set) and evaluating its performance on a held-out portion (the test set).

The "Evaluate Model" module provides a range of metrics for evaluating model performance, such as accuracy, precision, recall, F1-score, and AUC (Area Under the Curve). These metrics help us assess how well our model generalizes to unseen data. Based on the evaluation results, we can fine-tune the model's hyperparameters or try a different algorithm altogether. This iterative process of experimentation and refinement is inherent to machine learning, and Azure Machine Learning Studio simplifies this process through its visual interface and integrated evaluation tools.

Once we've identified a satisfactory model, we can deploy it using the "Web Service" module. This allows us to expose our model as a REST API, which other applications can then call to make predictions. This integration enables seamless integration into existing systems, making the model immediately actionable within the business context. The deployment process is streamlined in Azure

Machine
Learning Studio, with options for
various deployment targets including
cloud-based web services. The
platform handles the complexities of
deploying and scaling the model,
allowing us to focus on the model's
business impact.

Beyond the core functionalities, Azure
Machine Learning Studio offers
several additional benefits.
Collaboration features allow multiple
users to work on the same project
simultaneously, fostering teamwork
and knowledge sharing. Version
control features enable tracking
changes made to the experiment,
facilitating reproducibility and aiding
in
debugging. The integration with other
Azure services further extends the
platform's capabilities. For example,
the
integration with Azure Data Lake
Storage enables seamless access to
massive datasets for training larger
and more
complex models.

Consider another scenario: predicting housing prices. Here, our dataset might contain features like location, size, number

of bedrooms, and age of the property.
After importing the data, we could use
data transformation modules to handle
categorical features (like location)
using one-hot encoding or other
techniques. Numerical features like
size might require scaling or
normalization. We could explore
different
regression algorithms – linear
regression, polynomial
regression, or even support vector
regression – to find the model that
best predicts house prices. Model
evaluation would involve metrics such
as Mean Squared Error (MSE), R-
squared, and Root Mean Squared
Error (RMSE).
Deployment would again involve
creating a web service for making
predictions on new properties.

Let's also consider a scenario involving image
classification.
Suppose we want to build a model to
classify images of different types of

flowers. In this case, we would use modules designed for handling image data. We would likely leverage the power of pre-trained convolutional neural networks (CNNs) available within the platform, fine-tuning them using our flower dataset. This would significantly reduce the computational burden and the need for vast amounts of training data. The process would involve importing the image data, preprocessing it (resizing, normalization), training the CNN model, and then evaluating its performance using metrics like accuracy and precision. Deployment would follow the same pattern, enabling an image classification web service.

The power of Azure Machine Learning Studio lies not just in its ease of use but also in its scalability and integration with the broader Azure ecosystem. The platform can handle datasets of various sizes and complexities, scaling resources as needed. This is especially crucial when dealing with big data scenarios, where the sheer volume of data can pose challenges to traditional methods. The seamless integration with other Azure services, such as Azure Data Factory for

data integration and Azure Kubernetes Service for deploying models at scale, significantly amplifies the potential of the platform. The platform facilitates efficient collaboration and facilitates the entire lifecycle management of machine
learning models, from experimentation and testing to production deployment and monitoring. It's a valuable tool that empowers individuals with limited coding experience to build and deploy powerful machine learning models. This democratization of machine learning is a significant step forward, making the technology more accessible and widely applicable. Moreover, the platform's inherent support for responsible AI principles ensures that the models built are ethical, fair, and transparent. This blend of accessibility and responsible AI implementation solidifies Azure Machine Learning Studio's position

as a robust and valuable tool for the modern data scientist.

Utilizing Azures NoCodeLowCode AI Tools

Azure Machine Learning Studio, as discussed, provides a remarkable entry point into the world of machine learning for users with varying levels of coding expertise. However, it's just one piece of a larger, powerful puzzle within Azure's comprehensive AI ecosystem. Several other no-code and low-code tools complement Azure Machine Learning Studio, extending its capabilities and offering specialized functionalities for specific AI tasks. These tools cater to different needs and skill sets, further democratizing access to advanced AI capabilities.

One such powerful tool is **Azure AutoML**. While Azure Machine Learning Studio provides the flexibility to build custom models, AutoML automates a significant portion of the model building process. This is particularly beneficial when dealing with complex datasets and algorithms, where manual optimization can be time-consuming and require significant expertise. AutoML leverages cutting-edge

algorithms and techniques to automatically select the best model architecture and hyperparameters for a given task, thereby significantly reducing development time and effort. Imagine you're tasked with building a classification model to predict customer churn. With AutoML, you simply upload your data, specify the target variable (churn or no churn), and let the service do the rest. AutoML will explore various algorithms, such as logistic regression, support vector machines, and gradient boosting machines, and select the one that yields the best performance on your data. This automation not only saves time but also reduces the risk of human error during the model selection and tuning process.

Furthermore, AutoML provides comprehensive performance metrics and visualizations, allowing you to understand the

model's strengths and limitations. The automated feature engineering capabilities of AutoML deserve special mention.
AutoML intelligently selects and transforms relevant
features from your raw data, optimizing model performance. This greatly reduces the manual effort required for data preprocessing, a task that often consumes a significant portion of a data scientist's time. The ability to easily
compare the performance of different models trained by AutoML offers valuable insights for model selection and deployment. Its integration with Azure Machine Learning Workspace further streamlines the entire process, ensuring a seamless transition from model training to deployment.

Complementing AutoML's automation is

Azure Cognitive Services
. This suite of APIs provides pre-trained AI models for various cognitive tasks, such as image recognition, natural language processing, and speech recognition. Instead of building these models from scratch, developers can simply integrate these readily available APIs into their applications, dramatically reducing development time and cost. For instance, imagine you're developing a mobile app that allows users to identify plants using images. Instead of training a complex image recognition model, you can leverage Azure Cognitive Services' Computer Vision API, which already has pre-trained models capable of identifying a wide range of plant species. This approach requires minimal coding and focuses on integrating the existing, proven solution into your application. Similarly, for natural language processing tasks, the Text Analytics API can be used for sentiment analysis, key phrase extraction, and

language detection. For speech recognition, the Speech service converts spoken words into text, facilitating applications like voice assistants and transcription services. These services are scalable, reliable, and continually updated with the latest advancements in AI, ensuring that your applications benefit from state-of-the-art technology without requiring you to be a deep learning expert. The ease of integration with other Azure services further enhances the value of Cognitive Services. The low-code approach offered by Cognitive Services makes advanced AI capabilities readily accessible to a wider audience, fostering innovation and accelerating the development of AI-powered

applications. This is a significant departure from traditional approaches, which often necessitate extensive expertise in AI and machine learning algorithms.

Another valuable tool in Azure's no-code/low-code AI
arsenal is
Azure Bot Service
. This service simplifies the creation and deployment of conversational AI bots. It allows you to design bots using various channels, including Microsoft Teams, Facebook Messenger, and Slack, catering to

diverse user interfaces. Furthermore, the integration with the Bot Framework Composer provides a visual interface for designing conversational flows, allowing users to create bots without writing extensive code. Think of creating a customer service bot for your website. With Azure Bot Service, you can design the conversational flow visually, defining user intents and corresponding bot responses. The service handles the underlying infrastructure, scaling automatically to handle increasing user loads. The integration with other Azure services, like Cognitive Services for natural language understanding, further enhances the bot's capabilities. For instance, you can integrate the Language Understanding (LUIS) service to interpret user queries and the QnA Maker service to provide answers based on a knowledge base. This combination allows you to create sophisticated bots that can understand user intent and provide accurate, helpful responses. The ability to test and

monitor the bot's
performance from a centralized
dashboard is crucial for ensuring its
effectiveness and for continuous
improvement.
Azure Bot Service allows developers of all
skill levels to

build and deploy bots effectively, significantly lowering the barrier to entry for this increasingly important technology.

Beyond these primary tools, Azure offers a collection of other no-code and low-code resources that support the AI development lifecycle. These include pre-built solutions and templates tailored to specific industries and scenarios, eliminating the need for extensive development from scratch. This is particularly helpful for businesses looking to quickly implement AI solutions in their workflows. These pre-built solutions often come with comprehensive documentation and tutorials, further lowering the learning curve and encouraging wider adoption. The continuous updates and improvements made to these services ensure that users are always working with the latest AI technologies. Microsoft's commitment to responsible AI is embedded within these tools, ensuring fairness, transparency, and accountability in the development and deployment of AI solutions.

The synergy between these no-code/low-code tools and Azure Machine Learning Studio is noteworthy. While Azure Machine Learning Studio offers a flexible environment for building custom models, AutoML automates many aspects of this process. Cognitive Services provides pre-trained models for specific tasks, while Azure Bot Service allows the creation of conversational AI applications. These tools work in tandem, allowing users to select the most appropriate approach depending on their expertise and the specific requirements of their project. A data scientist proficient in coding might prefer using Azure Machine Learning Studio for complex custom model building, while a business analyst might find AutoML and

Cognitive Services more suitable for quickly deploying AI solutions. This flexibility and choice empower a wide range of users to leverage the power of AI, regardless of their technical expertise.

The availability of extensive documentation, tutorials, and community support further enhances the usability of these no-code/low-code tools. Microsoft's commitment to
providing comprehensive resources helps users overcome potential challenges and fully leverage the capabilities of these platforms. This creates a supportive ecosystem that fosters collaboration and accelerates innovation in the field of AI. The continuous updates and improvements to these tools ensure that users always have access to the latest advancements in AI technology. Microsoft's investment in research and development ensures that these platforms stay at the forefront of the field.

In conclusion, Azure's no-code/low-code AI tools represent a significant advancement in democratizing access to
artificial intelligence. By lowering the barriers to entry, these tools empower individuals and organizations with varying levels of technical expertise to develop and deploy powerful AI solutions. The combination of ease of use, scalability, and responsible AI principles solidifies Azure's position as a leading platform for AI innovation. The synergistic relationship between different platforms within Azure's ecosystem ensures that users can choose the most appropriate tools for their specific needs, maximizing
efficiency and effectiveness. This comprehensive suite of tools is not simply a collection of individual components but rather a cohesive ecosystem designed to empower a diverse range of users to harness the transformative power of
artificial intelligence. The future of AI development is likely to be characterized by a growing reliance on these types of tools, making

advanced capabilities more accessible
than ever before.

Deploying and Managing AI Models in Azure

Building upon our exploration of
Azure's no-code/low-code tools, the
next crucial step in your AI journey is
deploying and effectively managing
your trained models within the Azure
environment. This process goes
beyond simply
uploading a model; it involves a series
of strategic decisions and
configurations to ensure optimal
performance,
scalability, and security. Let's delve
into the practical aspects of deploying
and managing your AI models in
Azure.

One of the primary considerations is
choosing the
appropriate deployment target. Azure
offers several options, each with its
own strengths and weaknesses. For

simple deployments or models with lower inference requirements, Azure Machine Learning's online endpoints might suffice.

These endpoints allow for quick deployment and scaling, ideal for prototyping and testing. However, for production environments with high throughput and low latency demands, more robust solutions are necessary. Consider Azure Kubernetes Service (AKS) for containerized deployments, offering unparalleled scalability and flexibility.

AKS allows you to orchestrate containers holding your AI models, dynamically scaling resources based on real-time demand. This is particularly crucial for applications requiring rapid response times, such as real-time fraud detection or personalized recommendations. Choosing between these options depends critically on factors such as the complexity of your model, the expected traffic volume, and your budget. A small-scale application might thrive on online endpoints, while a large-scale, high-traffic application will undoubtedly benefit from the robust scalability of AKS.

Beyond the choice of deployment target, optimizing model performance is paramount. Model optimization techniques, such as quantization and pruning, can significantly reduce model size and improve inference speed. Quantization involves reducing the precision of model weights and activations, leading to smaller model sizes and faster processing. Pruning, on the other hand, involves removing less important connections within the neural network, further streamlining the model. Azure Machine Learning provides tools to facilitate these optimization processes, allowing you to fine-tune your models for optimal performance within your chosen deployment environment. Remember, the goal is not just to deploy your model but to deploy it efficiently, maximizing throughput while minimizing latency and resource consumption.

Experimentation with different optimization techniques is key to finding the optimal balance between model accuracy and performance. Thorough testing and benchmarking across various hardware configurations should be part of your optimization strategy.

Security is another critical aspect of deploying and managing AI models in Azure. Protecting your model from unauthorized access and ensuring data confidentiality are essential considerations. Azure offers several security
features to help you safeguard your AI assets. Azure's role-based access control (RBAC) allows you to granularly
control who has access to your models and resources. You can define specific roles with varying levels of permissions, ensuring that only authorized personnel can access or modify your models. Furthermore, integrating Azure's security
center provides continuous monitoring and threat detection, alerting you to potential vulnerabilities or suspicious

activities. Utilizing Virtual Networks (VNets) and private endpoints can further enhance security by isolating your AI infrastructure from public access. This approach ensures that only authorized internal components can interact with your

deployed models, minimizing the risk of external threats.
Regular security audits and penetration testing are also recommended to proactively identify and address potential vulnerabilities, ensuring the long-term integrity and security of your deployed AI systems.

Managing your deployed models goes beyond initial deployment. Monitoring their performance and addressing any issues that arise is essential for maintaining a reliable and effective AI system. Azure provides comprehensive monitoring tools to track model performance metrics, such as latency, throughput, and accuracy. By monitoring these key metrics, you can quickly identify potential problems such as model drift or performance degradation. Model drift refers to the phenomenon where a model's

accuracy
decreases over time due to changes
in the data distribution.
This is a common issue in real-world
applications,
necessitating regular model retraining
and updates. Azure Machine
Learning's automated machine
learning (AutoML) features can
simplify this process, automatically
retraining your models based on new
data and helping to maintain their
accuracy over time. Furthermore, the
ability to scale your model
deployments dynamically based on
real-time demand ensures that your AI
system can handle fluctuating
workloads without compromising
performance. This
scalability allows you to adjust
resources automatically, ensuring
optimal performance under various
conditions. By continuously
monitoring and adapting your
deployment strategy, you can ensure
the long-term effectiveness and
stability of your AI models within the
Azure environment.

Effective management also includes planning for model versioning and rollback capabilities. As your models evolve through retraining and optimization, maintaining a clear version history is crucial. Azure Machine Learning supports model versioning, enabling you to easily track changes and revert to previous versions if necessary. This functionality is particularly important when deploying models to production environments, allowing for seamless rollback in case of unforeseen issues or performance degradation. By meticulously managing model versions, you can ensure that your AI system remains stable and predictable. Thorough testing of each new version before deployment is also crucial to avoid disrupting existing functionalities. This iterative approach to deployment minimizes risks and maximizes the chance of a successful deployment.

Finally, cost optimization is a significant factor in managing AI models within Azure. Understanding the pricing structures for different Azure services and optimizing resource utilization are critical for maintaining a sustainable AI

infrastructure. Azure offers various pricing models,
including pay-as-you-go and reserved instances, allowing you to choose the option best suited to your needs and budget. By carefully monitoring resource consumption and right-sizing your deployments, you can minimize unnecessary expenditure. Utilizing Azure's cost management tools can provide valuable insights into your spending
patterns, enabling you to identify areas for potential cost savings. Remember that cost efficiency doesn't necessarily mean sacrificing performance; rather, it involves finding the optimal balance between resource utilization and performance requirements. Careful planning and monitoring of resource consumption are integral parts of long-term cost management.

In conclusion, deploying and managing AI models in Azure involves a multifaceted approach encompassing deployment target selection, model optimization, security measures, performance monitoring, version control, and cost optimization. By thoughtfully considering these aspects and leveraging Azure's comprehensive suite of tools and services, you can effectively deploy and manage your AI models, ensuring optimal performance, scalability, security, and cost-efficiency. This holistic approach to AI model deployment transforms your AI projects from isolated experiments into reliable, scalable, and secure production systems, maximizing the value of your investments in AI. Remember that continuous learning and adaptation are vital for staying abreast of best practices and maximizing the return on your AI deployments within the ever-evolving landscape of Azure's AI ecosystem. The journey doesn't end with deployment; it's an ongoing process of refinement and optimization, constantly striving for better performance, security, and efficiency.

Review of Key Concepts and Exam Strategies

This chapter concludes our journey through the world of AI and the Microsoft Azure AI services. Before you confidently tackle the AI-900 exam, let's reinforce the core concepts and equip you with effective strategies for exam success. This isn't just about memorizing facts; it's about understanding the underlying principles and how they interconnect.

We've covered a vast landscape, starting with the fundamental definitions of artificial intelligence, machine learning, and deep learning. Remember the crucial distinctions between narrow, general, and super AI – understanding these differences is vital for comprehending the limitations and potential of current AI technologies. We explored the three main categories of machine learning: supervised, unsupervised, and reinforcement learning. Recall the key characteristics of each, including the type of data used for training and the goals of each approach. Think back to the examples we discussed – predicting customer churn using supervised learning, clustering customer segments using unsupervised learning, and training a robot to navigate a maze using reinforcement learning. These examples were designed to illustrate the practical application of these fundamental concepts.

The core algorithms – regression, classification, and clustering – are crucial building blocks. Visualize the processes; imagine the data points being grouped in clustering, the line of best fit in regression, and the decision boundaries separating classes in classification. Understanding these visual representations will greatly assist your comprehension. Furthermore, the chapter on anomaly detection provided insight into identifying unusual patterns within datasets. This technique has far-reaching implications in fraud detection, cybersecurity, and predictive maintenance, underscoring the practical impact of AI.

Our exploration of computer vision introduced you to image classification, object detection, and image segmentation. Recall the various Azure services we discussed, including the Computer Vision API, the Face API, and Form Recognizer. Think of real-world applications – imagine using these services to automate image tagging in a social media platform, analyzing facial expressions in a marketing campaign, or extracting information from documents.

Natural Language Processing (NLP) was another critical area. Remember the key tasks of NLP, such as text classification, sentiment analysis, named entity recognition, and language translation. Again, relate these back to real-world applications – building a chatbot that understands natural language, analyzing customer reviews to gauge product sentiment, or creating a multilingual translation service. We explored Azure's offerings in this space, including Text Analytics, LUIS, Speech Service, and Translator. Try to visualize the workflows involved in each of these services.

The creation and utilization of conversational AI using Azure Bot Service and Bot Framework Composer were also explored. Think of the design considerations when building an effective and engaging chatbot – clear intent recognition, personalized responses, and a seamless user experience. Remember how we integrated other Azure AI services to enhance chatbot functionality.

Responsible AI is not just a buzzword; it's a critical element.

Reflect on Microsoft's six principles of responsible AI: fairness, reliability, privacy, inclusiveness, transparency, and accountability. These aren't abstract concepts; they are essential considerations in every stage of the AI lifecycle, from data collection and model training to deployment and monitoring. Consider the ethical implications and the potential for bias in AI systems, and the methods to mitigate those risks. We discussed data preprocessing techniques, algorithm selection, and post-processing methods to address these challenges.

Our foray into Azure Machine Learning and its no-code/low-code tools offered a practical pathway to build and deploy AI solutions. Recall the capabilities of Azure Machine Learning Studio and Azure AutoML – tools that empower both programmers and non-programmers to build and deploy machine learning models. Visualize the steps involved in using these platforms, from data preparation to model deployment. Remember the importance of scalability, performance, and security when deploying and managing AI models in Azure.

To prepare effectively for the AI-900 exam, focus on a structured approach. First, review the official exam objectives, ensuring you understand each one thoroughly. Create a comprehensive study plan that allocates sufficient time to each topic, incorporating regular review sessions and practice questions.

Don't just passively read the material; actively engage with it. Take notes, draw diagrams, and create your own examples. Focus on understanding the "why" behind concepts, not just the "what." Understanding the underlying principles will help you answer a wider range of questions.

Utilize the practice questions provided in this book and supplement them with additional practice materials available online. These practice questions aren't just for testing your knowledge; they are opportunities to identify your weak areas and focus your study efforts. Simulate the exam environment as much as possible – time yourself and practice under pressure to build your exam stamina.

Remember the importance of time management during the exam. Read each question carefully, avoid spending too much time on any single question, and make sure you answer all the questions within the allotted time. Maintain a calm and focused demeanor on exam day. Get a good night's sleep, eat a healthy meal, and arrive early to minimize stress.

Upon passing the AI-900 exam, your journey continues. Consider pursuing further certifications, such as the Azure AI Engineer Associate certification, to deepen your expertise. Explore online courses, attend workshops, join professional communities, and stay updated on the latest advancements in the field. The AI landscape is constantly evolving, and continuous learning is key to staying ahead.

This book has provided you with a strong foundation in AI and Azure AI services. Remember, the key to success isn't just about passing an exam; it's about cultivating a deep understanding of the principles, continuously learning, and applying your knowledge to solve real-world problems. Embrace the opportunities this field offers, and confidently navigate the exciting world of artificial intelligence. Good luck with your exam! Now go and conquer! Remember to refer back to the earlier chapters and the glossary for any terms or concepts that need further clarification. Consistent review and application of the knowledge gained will significantly enhance your chances of exam success. Don't hesitate to utilize the free tier of Azure to experiment further with the services we've covered. Hands-on experience will solidify your understanding and prepare you for the practical aspects of AI development. The key is to keep practicing, keep learning, and to keep applying what you have learned.

Practice Exam Questions and Answers

Now, let's put your knowledge to the test with a series of practice exam questions designed to mirror the style and difficulty of the AI-900 exam. Remember, understanding the *why* behind the answer is just as crucial as getting the correct answer itself. Each question is followed by a detailed explanation, designed to reinforce key concepts and address potential misconceptions. Take your time, review the relevant chapters if needed, and don't hesitate to revisit the glossary for any terminology that requires clarification. This practice is vital for solidifying your understanding and building confidence for the actual exam.

Practice Exam Questions and Answers:

1. Which of the following best describes Artificial Narrow Intelligence (ANI)?

a) AI capable of performing any intellectual task a human being can.
b) AI that surpasses human intelligence in all aspects. c) AI specialized to perform a single task or a narrow range of tasks.
d) AI with self-awareness and consciousness.

Answer: c) AI specialized to perform a single task or a narrow range of tasks.

Explanation:
ANI, also known as Weak AI, is the most prevalent type of AI today. It excels in specific tasks, like playing chess or recommending products, but lacks the general intelligence of a human. Options a, b, and d describe Artificial General Intelligence (AGI) and Artificial

Superintelligence (ASI), which
are currently theoretical concepts.

**2. What type of machine learning
algorithm is best suited for
predicting a continuous value, such
as house prices?**

a
)

C
l
a
s
s
i
f
i
c
a
t
i
o
n

b)

Clustering

c)

Regression

d)

Anomaly Detection

Answer: c) Regression

Explanation:
Regression algorithms are designed to predict a continuous output variable based on one or more input variables. Linear regression, polynomial regression, and support vector regression are examples of regression algorithms. Classification deals with categorical outputs, clustering groups

similar data points, and anomaly detection identifies outliers.

3. Which Azure service is primarily used for extracting text from images?

a) Azure Cognitive Search
b) Azure Bot Service
c) Azure Computer Vision
d)

Azur
e
Mac
hine
Lear
ning

Answer: c) Azure Computer Vision

Explanation:
Azure Computer Vision offers
Optical
Character Recognition (OCR)
capabilities, allowing it to extract
text from images and convert it into
machine-
readable format. While Azure
Cognitive Search can index images,
it doesn't directly perform OCR.
Azure Bot Service

and Azure Machine Learning are focused on different AI capabilities.

4. What is the primary purpose of Natural Language Processing (NLP)?

a) To enable machines to understand and interpret human language.
b) To generate realistic images from text descriptions. c) To detect anomalies in data streams.
d) To manage and analyze large datasets.

Answer: a) To enable machines to understand and interpret human language.

Explanation:
NLP focuses on enabling computers to understand, interpret, and generate human language. This includes tasks like sentiment

analysis, text summarization, machine translation, and chatbot development.

5. Which of the following is NOT a core principle of responsible AI as promoted by Microsoft?

a
)

F
a
i
r
n
e
s
s

b
)

R
e
l
i
a
b

ility

c) Profit Maximization

d

)

Transparency

Answer: c) Profit Maximization

Explanation:
While profitability is a business consideration, it should not be prioritized over ethical considerations. Microsoft's responsible AI principles prioritize fairness, reliability, privacy, inclusiveness, transparency, and accountability. Profit maximization alone can lead to biased or harmful AI systems.

6. What is the purpose of Azure AutoML?

a) To manually code complex machine learning models. b) To automate the process of creating and deploying machine learning models.
c) To manage virtual machines in Azure.
d) To build and deploy chatbots.

Answer: b) To automate the process of creating and deploying machine learning models.

Explanation:
Azure AutoML simplifies the process of building machine learning models by automating many steps, including data preparation, model selection, training, and deployment. This makes machine learning accessible to users with less coding expertise.

7. Which Azure service is best suited for building conversational AI applications?

a) Azure Cognitive Search

b) Azure Machine Learning

c) Azure Bot Service

d) Azure Com

pute
r
Visi
on

Answer: c) Azure Bot Service

Explanation:
Azure Bot Service provides a comprehensive platform for building, testing, and deploying intelligent chatbots. It integrates with other Azure services like LUIS (Language Understanding Intelligent Service) and QnA Maker.

8. Explain the difference between supervised, unsupervised, and reinforcement learning.

Answer:

Supervised Learning:
This approach involves training a model on a labeled dataset, where each data point is associated with a known output. The model learns to map inputs to outputs based on this labeled data. Examples include image classification and spam detection.

Unsupervised Learning:
In this case, the model is trained on an unlabeled dataset, meaning there are no known outputs. The model aims to discover patterns, structures, or relationships within the data. Clustering and dimensionality reduction are common unsupervised learning techniques.

Reinforcement Learning:
This type of learning involves an

agent that interacts with an
environment and learns to make
decisions to maximize a reward. The
agent learns through trial and error,
receiving feedback in the form of
rewards or penalties. Examples
include game playing and robotics
control.

9. Describe the role of bias in AI and how to mitigate it.

Answer:
Bias in AI refers to systematic errors
in a model's output that are due to
biases present in the training data or
the model's design. These biases can
perpetuate and amplify existing
societal inequalities. For example, a
facial
recognition system trained on
predominantly white faces might
perform poorly on faces of other
ethnicities.

Mitigating bias requires a multi-faceted
approach:

Careful Data Collection:
Ensuring the training data is

diverse, representative, and free from biases.

Algorithmic Fairness:
Developing algorithms that are less
susceptible to bias.
**Regular Auditing and
Monitoring:**
Continuously monitoring the
model's performance across
different demographic groups
to detect and address bias.
Explainable AI (XAI):
Understanding the reasoning behind a
model's decisions to identify and
correct biases.
Human Oversight:
Incorporating human review
and intervention to prevent
harmful biases.

**10. What are some key
considerations for ensuring the
privacy and security of data used
in AI projects?**

Answer:
Data privacy and security are
critical aspects of responsible AI

development. Key considerations
include:

Data Minimization:
Collecting only the necessary data
for the AI task.
Data Anonymization:
Removing or transforming
identifying information to protect
individuals' privacy. **Data
Encryption:**
Protecting data both in transit and at
rest using encryption techniques.
Access Control:
Implementing strict access control
measures to limit who can access
and modify the data. **Compliance
with Regulations:**
Adhering to relevant data privacy
regulations, such as GDPR and
CCPA.
Security Monitoring:
Regularly monitoring the system for
security breaches and vulnerabilities.

These practice questions provide a
strong foundation for your AI-900
exam preparation. Remember to
continue reviewing the concepts
covered in the previous chapters and

actively experiment with Azure's free tier services to
reinforce your practical understanding. Consistent effort and a deep understanding of the underlying principles will
significantly improve your chances of success. Good luck!

Remember, passing the exam is a significant accomplishment, but it's merely the beginning of your journey in the dynamic world of artificial intelligence. Continue learning, exploring, and innovating!

Tips for Success on Exam Day

The culmination of your diligent preparation is here: exam day. While the knowledge you've acquired through studying this book and engaging with Azure's resources forms the bedrock of your success, effective exam-taking strategies can significantly enhance your performance. This isn't just about recalling facts; it's about demonstrating a comprehensive understanding of AI principles and Azure's AI services.

Firstly, let's address time management. The AI-900 exam is designed to test your knowledge within a specific timeframe. Before you even begin answering questions, take a few moments to survey the entire exam. Note the number of questions and their respective point values, if applicable. This preliminary scan helps you gauge the overall scope and allocate your time proportionally. Avoid spending too much time on any single question, especially those you find initially challenging. Mark those questions for review and move on. You can always return to them later if time permits. A strategic approach involves focusing on the questions you know you can answer accurately and efficiently first, building momentum and confidence.

Remember, the exam isn't a race; it's a test of your understanding. A common mistake is rushing through questions, leading to careless errors and missed opportunities to demonstrate your expertise. Pace yourself calmly and deliberately. Read each question carefully, paying attention to keywords and nuances. Underline or highlight key phrases to ensure you're addressing the core of the question.

Misinterpreting a question can lead to choosing the wrong answer, even if you possess the correct knowledge. Take a deep breath if you feel overwhelmed or stressed. Short, controlled breaths can help regulate your nervous system and enhance focus.

Stress management is paramount. On the day of the exam, try to maintain a calm and composed demeanor. A stressful mental state can impair cognitive function, hindering your ability to recall information and solve problems effectively. Techniques like deep breathing exercises, mindfulness meditation, or even a short walk before the exam can help alleviate anxiety. Remember the preparation you've undertaken; trust in your knowledge and abilities. You've invested time and effort in reaching this point; now is the time to showcase your learning.

Prioritize understanding over memorization. While rote learning might seem like a shortcut, a true understanding of the underlying

concepts is far more valuable during the exam. The AI-900 exam tests your comprehension of AI principles and your ability to apply that knowledge to
practical scenarios involving Azure services. Focus on grasping the "why" behind the algorithms and the functionality of Azure's AI tools. This approach not only improves your chances of answering questions correctly but also allows you to approach unfamiliar questions with greater confidence. If you encounter a question involving a service you haven't extensively used, try to deduce the answer by applying your foundational knowledge of AI concepts and the general functionality of Azure services.

Employ elimination techniques. If you're unsure of the
correct answer, strategically eliminate obviously wrong options. This narrows down the possibilities and improves your odds of selecting the correct response. Even if you can't confidently identify the correct answer immediately,

eliminating incorrect choices
significantly increases your chances
of success through educated guessing.
Review your

choices carefully before submitting your final answer. A small amount of careful consideration can make a significant difference in improving accuracy.

During the exam, maintain a positive mindset. Negative self-talk can be detrimental to your performance. Instead, focus on your strengths and your preparedness. Visualize your success; this mental imagery can boost your confidence and improve your focus. Believe in your abilities and trust your preparation. This is a crucial step for success on exam day and beyond.

Beyond the individual questions, consider the bigger picture.
The AI-900 exam isn't just about passing; it's about demonstrating your competence in a rapidly growing field.
The knowledge you've gained will be invaluable in your future career in AI.

Remember that successful completion of the exam is a testament to your dedication and hard work. Celebrate your accomplishment; you've achieved a significant milestone.

Let's delve deeper into specific strategies for tackling different question types. Multiple-choice questions, a staple of many certification exams, require careful consideration of all options. Don't jump to conclusions; read every choice thoroughly before making a selection. Pay close attention to any qualifiers like "always," "never," "usually," or "sometimes," as these words can significantly alter the meaning of a statement. Eliminate obviously incorrect options, and then carefully consider the remaining choices. If you're unsure, try to recall relevant information from the chapters of this book or your notes.

Scenario-based questions often present a realistic problem and require you to choose the best solution from a list of options. These questions test your practical understanding of

AI concepts and Azure services. Read the scenario carefully and identify the key challenges or requirements. Then, analyze each option, considering its feasibility, effectiveness, and alignment with best practices. It's useful to try and break down the problem into smaller, more manageable components. This can clarify the exact requirements and make it easier to identify the optimal solution.

Matching questions will require you to pair concepts, services, or functionalities. To approach these effectively, consider the relationships between items in each list. Start by identifying the most obvious matches, and then systematically work your way through the remaining items. This approach helps in building confidence and ensuring you don't overlook less obvious connections. If you're uncertain about a particular match, consider the context and the broader concepts associated with the items. This can aid you in making an informed judgment.

Remember, the exam is designed to assess your understanding, not to trick you. While the questions might present challenges, they are primarily focused on testing your knowledge and practical application of AI concepts and Azure services. Approach each question calmly, thoughtfully, and methodically.

After the exam, take some time for self-reflection. Regardless of the outcome, analyze your performance. If you didn't achieve the desired score, identify areas where your understanding was lacking. Use this as a learning opportunity; it's a valuable part of your development as an AI professional. Review the exam objectives, focusing on areas where you struggled. This will help you pinpoint gaps in your knowledge and tailor your future study efforts more effectively.

Microsoft provides comprehensive resources and feedback mechanisms for those taking their certifications. Leverage these resources to understand the areas where you excelled and where you might need additional learning. Engage in online communities and forums; sharing experiences and learning from others' journeys can be incredibly beneficial.
This feedback can help refine your study approach and enhance your understanding for future endeavors.

Success in the AI-900 exam requires dedication, effective study habits, and intelligent test-taking strategies. By integrating these tips and maintaining a positive and focused approach, you significantly enhance your chances of achieving your goal. Remember, the exam is a checkpoint, not an endpoint. The journey into the world of AI is ongoing, and this exam is merely a step on a far more expansive path. Embrace the challenges, learn from setbacks, and continuously strive for greater understanding and expertise. The world of AI is constantly evolving, and continuous learning is key to maintaining a competitive edge.

Further Learning Resources and Continuing Education

Beyond the AI-900 exam lies a vast and ever-evolving landscape of opportunities within the field of Artificial Intelligence. Passing the exam is a significant accomplishment, marking a milestone in your AI journey, but it's just the beginning. Continuous learning and professional development are crucial for staying abreast of the latest advancements and maintaining a competitive edge in this rapidly changing field. This section explores a variety of resources to support your ongoing learning and career progression.

One of the most valuable resources for continued learning is the wealth of online courses available from various

platforms. Microsoft Learn, for example, offers numerous courses specifically designed to expand your knowledge of Azure AI services and related technologies. These courses cover various skill levels, from introductory materials
reinforcing the concepts covered in this book to advanced courses exploring specialized techniques and applications.
They often include hands-on labs and practical exercises, allowing you to solidify your understanding and gain
practical experience. Many courses offer certifications upon completion, providing tangible evidence of your skill
development.

Beyond Microsoft Learn, platforms like Coursera, edX, Udacity, and Udemy provide a wide range of AI-related courses. These courses often cover specific aspects of AI, such as deep learning, natural language processing, computer vision, or reinforcement learning, allowing you to specialize in areas that align with your interests and career goals. You can explore courses taught by leading experts in the field, gaining exposure to cutting-edge research and practical applications. Many of these platforms offer flexible learning options, allowing you to learn at your own pace and schedule, accommodating different learning styles and busy schedules.

Furthermore, several universities and institutions offer specialized online master's programs and certifications in AI and related fields. These programs provide a more structured and in-depth learning experience, often culminating in a formal degree or certification. These programs can significantly enhance your career prospects, showcasing a deeper commitment to the field and a higher level of expertise.

While online courses provide structured learning paths, actively engaging with the AI community can significantly boost your learning and professional development.

Participating in online forums and communities allows you to connect with other AI enthusiasts, professionals, and experts. Platforms like Stack Overflow, Reddit (specifically subreddits focused on AI and machine learning), and Discord servers dedicated to AI discussions provide opportunities to ask questions, share knowledge, and collaborate on projects. These interactions expose you to diverse perspectives, problem-solving approaches, and real-world challenges faced by AI practitioners. Engaging in these communities fosters a collaborative learning environment, encouraging the exchange of ideas and the development of problem-solving skills.

Attending AI conferences and workshops is another excellent avenue for continuous learning. These events provide opportunities to network with industry leaders, learn about the latest advancements from researchers and practitioners, and gain hands-on experience with new technologies. Conferences often feature keynote speeches, technical presentations, workshops, and networking events, creating an immersive learning experience. The exposure to cutting-edge research and emerging trends keeps you informed and provides context for the rapidly evolving landscape of AI.

Beyond formal learning, continuous self-study plays a critical role in professional development within AI. Regularly reading research papers, articles, and industry blogs can expose you to the latest breakthroughs and best practices. Websites such as arXiv and publications from leading AI research groups provide access to cutting-edge research findings. Following industry blogs and publications helps you stay informed about practical applications and industry trends. Actively searching for and reading relevant content helps you cultivate a deep understanding and keep up with rapid developments within the field.

Moreover, actively engaging in personal projects is a powerful method for enhancing your AI skills. This allows you to apply the theoretical knowledge you've gained through courses and research to practical problem-solving. Consider working on projects that interest you, whether it's developing a simple machine learning model, creating a chatbot, or building a computer vision application. Projects allow you to deepen your understanding of specific technologies and gain practical experience that enhances your resume and demonstrates your skillset to potential employers.

The development of your portfolio should be a consistent part of your continued professional development. As you complete personal projects, ensure you meticulously

document your process, including
your approach, challenges

encountered, solutions implemented, and results obtained.

This documentation serves as valuable evidence of your skills and abilities. When applying for jobs or seeking career advancement, a strong portfolio showcasing your practical experience and problem-solving abilities greatly enhances your chances of success. It provides tangible evidence of your capabilities, allowing potential employers to assess your skills and experience firsthand. Platforms like GitHub are ideal for showcasing your code and project details, making it readily accessible to potential employers and collaborators.

In addition to enhancing your technical expertise, building strong communication skills is vital for success in the AI field. Effectively communicating complex technical concepts to both technical and non-technical audiences is a key skill for many roles within AI. Practicing your presentation skills through participation in conferences, workshops, or even informal presentations within your network helps you refine your ability to convey information concisely and engagingly.

The pursuit of additional certifications can also significantly boost your career prospects. While the AI-900 certification serves as a foundational step, several other Microsoft certifications, such as those focusing on Azure Machine Learning or specific AI services, can demonstrate advanced skills and specialization. Consider pursuing these certifications to highlight your expertise in specific areas and to demonstrate your ongoing commitment to professional development. These certifications serve as valuable credentials, bolstering your resume and attracting the attention of employers seeking individuals with advanced skills.

Finally, remember that networking is a crucial component of professional development. Attend industry events, join

online communities, and reach out to professionals in the field. Building relationships with other AI professionals can provide invaluable support, mentorship, and opportunities.
These connections can lead to collaborations, job
opportunities, and valuable insights into the latest trends and advancements in the field.

The journey into the world of AI is continuous. The AI-900 exam is a stepping stone, not the destination. By actively engaging in these learning resources and cultivating a commitment to continuous professional development, you will not only maintain a competitive edge but also enjoy a rewarding and fulfilling career in this rapidly growing field. The key is to embrace the ongoing learning process, adapt to new technologies, and continuously strive for growth and advancement.

The AI landscape is constantly evolving, and your commitment to continuous learning will be the key to navigating its exciting future.

Glossary of Key Terms

This glossary provides concise definitions for key terms and concepts discussed throughout this book, serving as a
valuable reference as you continue your journey into the world of artificial intelligence. Understanding these terms is crucial for both passing the AI-900 exam and succeeding in a career focused on AI.

Accuracy:
In the context of machine learning models,
accuracy refers to the percentage of correct predictions made by the model. A higher accuracy signifies a more reliable model. It's important to note that accuracy alone may not be a sufficient metric; other metrics like precision and recall should also be considered, especially when dealing

with imbalanced datasets. For example, a model predicting fraud might have high accuracy by correctly identifying most non-fraudulent transactions, but it could fail to identify a significant portion of fraudulent ones – a critical flaw.

Algorithm:
A set of rules and statistical techniques used by a computer to solve a problem or perform a specific task. In machine learning, algorithms are the core components that enable learning from data. Different algorithms are suitable for different tasks and data types; choosing the right algorithm is crucial for model performance. Examples include linear regression, logistic regression, support vector machines, and decision trees. The selection often involves considerations of data size, dimensionality, and the nature of the problem (classification, regression, clustering).

AI (Artificial Intelligence):
The simulation of human
intelligence processes by
machines, especially computer
systems. These processes include
learning (acquiring

information and rules for using the information), reasoning (using rules to reach approximate or definite conclusions), and self-correction. AI encompasses various subfields like machine learning, deep learning, natural language processing, and computer vision. The field is constantly evolving, moving beyond narrow, task-specific AI to more general, adaptable systems.

Anomaly Detection:
The process of identifying data points or events that deviate significantly from the norm. These anomalies can indicate errors, fraudulent activity, or other noteworthy occurrences. Anomaly detection techniques range from statistical methods to machine learning
algorithms, and their effectiveness heavily depends on the type and

characteristics of the data being analyzed.

Examples include detecting credit card fraud or identifying faulty equipment in a manufacturing process. Different approaches are suitable for different data types (e.g., time series, network data) and anomaly characteristics.

Azure Machine Learning (AML):
Microsoft's cloud-based platform for building, training, and deploying machine learning models. AML provides tools for data preparation, model building, experimentation, and deployment, making the process significantly more efficient. Its integrated capabilities, including AutoML, simplify the development process for users with varying levels of expertise.

Azure AutoML:
A component of Azure Machine Learning that automates the process of building machine learning models. AutoML simplifies the model selection, hyperparameter tuning, and training

processes, making it accessible even to users with limited machine learning expertise. It's invaluable for quickly creating models for various tasks, particularly when dealing with datasets that don't require extensive manual feature engineering.

However, AutoML might not always achieve the optimal performance compared to a manually tuned model for complex tasks.

Bias in AI:
Systematic errors in a machine learning model that result from skewed or incomplete training data. These biases can lead to unfair or discriminatory outcomes, reflecting existing biases present in the data. Addressing bias requires careful data collection, preprocessing, and model evaluation techniques. Identifying and mitigating bias is a crucial aspect of responsible AI development. Examples include facial recognition systems showing higher error rates for certain ethnic groups, or loan applications algorithms disproportionately rejecting applications from specific demographics.

Bot Framework Composer:
A visual development tool for building conversational AI bots. It provides a low-code/no-code approach to bot creation, making it accessible to
developers with different levels of experience. This tool enables designing conversational flows, integrating with various services, and testing the bot's interactions.

Classification:
A machine learning task where the goal is to assign data points to predefined categories or classes. For example, classifying emails as spam or not spam, or
identifying images of cats versus dogs. Various classification algorithms exist, such as logistic regression, support vector machines, and decision trees, each with its strengths and weaknesses. The choice depends on the dataset characteristics and the desired level of accuracy and interpretability.

Clustering:
A machine learning task that groups similar data points together based on their inherent characteristics. Unlike classification, clustering doesn't use predefined

categories; instead, it discovers inherent groupings within the data. K-means clustering and hierarchical clustering are common clustering algorithms. The selection of a clustering algorithm depends on the data structure, the desired number of clusters, and the interpretation goals.

Computer Vision:
A field of AI that enables computers to "see" and interpret images and videos. It involves techniques for image recognition, object detection, and image segmentation. Microsoft Azure provides several services for computer vision tasks, including the Computer Vision service, Face service, and Form Recognizer.

Conversational AI:
The development of systems that can engage in natural and meaningful conversations with

humans. Conversational AI leverages natural language processing (NLP) and machine learning to understand user input, generate appropriate responses, and manage the conversation flow. Examples include chatbots, virtual assistants, and interactive voice response systems.

Data Science:
An interdisciplinary field that uses scientific methods, processes, algorithms, and systems to extract knowledge and insights from structured and unstructured data. Data science involves a variety of techniques, including data mining, machine learning, and statistics, and is applied in many fields to solve problems and make decisions.

Deep Learning:
A subfield of machine learning that uses artificial neural networks with multiple layers (hence "deep") to analyze data. Deep learning has achieved remarkable success in areas like image recognition, natural language processing, and speech

recognition. The complexity of deep learning models often requires significant computational resources.

Explainable AI (XAI):
A field focused on making the decision-making processes of AI models more transparent and understandable. XAI addresses the "black box" problem inherent in some AI models, enabling users to understand how a model arrived at a specific prediction. This transparency is crucial for building trust and ensuring responsible AI development.

Fairness (in AI):
The principle of ensuring that AI systems treat all individuals and groups equitably, avoiding discriminatory outcomes. Achieving fairness in AI requires careful consideration of data biases, model design, and deployment strategies.

Feature Engineering:
The process of selecting, transforming, and creating features from raw data to improve the

performance of machine learning models. Feature
engineering is a crucial step that significantly impacts model accuracy and efficiency. It involves selecting relevant
attributes, creating new ones from existing ones, and
applying transformations to improve model training and predictive accuracy.

Generative AI:

A type of AI that can generate new content, such as text, images, or audio. Generative models learn patterns from existing data and use these patterns to create new data similar in style and content.

Hyperparameter Tuning:

The process of optimizing the parameters of a machine learning model that control the learning process itself, rather than the parameters learned from the data. Hyperparameter tuning is crucial for achieving optimal model performance. Different techniques are used to find optimal hyperparameter settings, including grid search, random search, and Bayesian optimization.

Machine Learning (ML):
A subfield of AI that focuses on enabling computer systems to learn from data without being explicitly programmed. Machine learning algorithms learn patterns from data and use these patterns to make predictions or decisions.

Microsoft Cognitive Services:
A suite of cloud-based AI services offered by Microsoft that provide pre-trained
models for various AI tasks, including computer vision, speech recognition, natural language processing, and knowledge mining. These services simplify the development of AI applications.

Model Deployment:
The process of making a trained machine learning model available for use in a real-world application. Deployment involves deploying the model to a suitable environment,

integrating it with other systems, and ensuring its performance and scalability.

Natural Language Processing (NLP):
A field of AI focused on enabling computers to understand, interpret, and generate human language. NLP involves techniques for text analysis, sentiment analysis, machine translation, and chatbot development. Microsoft Azure offers various NLP services, including the Text Analytics service, Language Understanding (LUIS), Speech service, and Translator.

Precision:
In machine learning, precision measures the proportion of correctly predicted positive cases among all instances predicted as positive. It's especially relevant when the cost of false positives is high.

Recall:
In machine learning, recall measures the proportion of correctly predicted

positive cases among all actual positive cases. It highlights the model's ability to identify all positive instances. A high recall is crucial when missing positive cases is costly.

Reinforcement Learning:
A type of machine learning where an agent learns to interact with an environment by receiving rewards or penalties for its actions. The agent learns a policy that maximizes its cumulative reward over time.

Responsible AI:
The development and deployment of AI systems in a way that aligns with ethical principles, promotes fairness, and addresses potential risks. Responsible AI emphasizes transparency, accountability, and inclusivity.

Supervised   Learning:
A type of machine learning where the algorithm learns from labeled data, meaning each data point is

associated with a known outcome or label.
Supervised learning is used for tasks like classification and regression.

Unsupervised Learning:
A type of machine learning where the algorithm learns from unlabeled data, meaning there are no known outcomes or labels associated with the data points.
Unsupervised learning is used for tasks like clustering and anomaly detection.

Azure QnA Maker:
A service in Microsoft Azure that allows you to create conversational AI chatbots from existing knowledge bases, such as FAQs, documents, and product manuals. It facilitates easy chatbot development by automatically generating answers based on the provided content.

These definitions provide a strong foundation for your continued study of AI. Remember that the AI landscape is ever-evolving, and continuous learning is vital for staying current with the latest developments and best practices. By grasping these key concepts, you're well-positioned to succeed in your AI journey.

Acknowledgments

Writing a book is rarely a solitary endeavor, and this one is no exception. I extend my deepest gratitude to [List names and affiliations of individuals who provided significant contributions, e.g., technical reviewers, editors, family, friends]. Their insights, feedback, and unwavering support were instrumental in shaping this book into its final form.
Special thanks to [Name] for [Specific contribution, e.g., their invaluable expertise in Azure AI services], and to [Name] for [Specific contribution, e.g., their meticulous editing and patience]. Finally, I want to thank my family for their understanding and encouragement throughout this challenging but rewarding process.

Any errors or omissions remain
solely my responsibility.

Appendix

This appendix provides supplementary materials to enhance your understanding of the concepts discussed in this book. It includes:

List of Azure AI Services and their Key Features:
A table summarizing the various Azure AI services covered, outlining their core functionalities, and providing links to relevant Microsoft documentation.

Additional Practice Questions:
A collection of additional practice questions to further solidify your understanding of the exam objectives. Answers are provided at the end of this section.

Links to Relevant Microsoft Documentation:
A curated list of links to official Microsoft documentation on AI

concepts, Azure services, and responsible AI principles.

Glossary

AI (Artificial Intelligence):
The simulation of human intelligence processes by machines, especially computer systems. These processes include learning, reasoning, and self-correction.

Machine Learning (ML):
A subset of AI where systems learn from data without explicit programming. This involves algorithms that identify patterns, make predictions, and improve their accuracy over time.

Deep Learning (DL):
A subset of ML that uses artificial neural networks with multiple layers to analyze data and extract complex patterns.

Supervised Learning:
A type of ML where algorithms learn from labeled data, meaning the data includes both input features and the corresponding output or target variable.

Unsupervised Learning:
A type of ML where algorithms learn from unlabeled data, identifying patterns and structures without predefined outputs.

Reinforcement Learning:
A type of ML where algorithms learn through trial and error, receiving rewards or penalties based on their actions.

Natural Language Processing (NLP):
A branch of AI focusing on enabling computers to understand, interpret, and generate human language.

Computer Vision:
A field of AI that enables computers to "see" and interpret images and videos.

Azure Machine Learning:
Microsoft's cloud-based
platform for building, training,
and deploying machine learning
models.

**AutoML (Automated Machine
Learning):**
A set of tools and services that
automate the process of building
machine learning models, making it
accessible to users with limited
coding experience.

**(Include other relevant terms and their
definitions.)**

www.ingramcontent.com/pod-product-compliance
Lightning Source LLC
LaVergne TN
LVHW022332060326
832902LV00022B/4004